# LEARNING TO LEAD FOR THE KINGDOM

A call for a deeper understanding of the
message of Jesus

**EMMANUEL NGARA**

Unless otherwise identified: All scripture quotations, are taken from the New International Version (NIV) of the Holy Bible. Copyright © 1973, 1978, 1984, 2011 by Biblica, Inc. Used by permission. Italics used on scripture is for emphasis only.

Copyright © 2020 Emmanuel Ngara
Learning to lead for the Kingdom
ISBN: 978-0-620-91407-9


Cover design: Stanley Maake
Published by: Nolo Publishers
Typeset in 12/13 Garamond by Stanley Maake
Printed by Nolo Publishers 1 2 3 4 5 1 2

**≡NOLO**
**Publishers**

Every effort has been made to obtain copyright permission for the material used in this book. Please contact the author with any queries in this regard.

# Dedication

This book is dedicated to Brother Roger (Roger Louis Schutz-Marsauche: 1915-2005), the Founder of the Taize Community. I never knew Brother Roger, but have been inspired by his total commitment to ecumenism, his spirit of openness to all Christians, and his dedicated service to the poor and suffering, especially those who found themselves as victims during the Second World War.

I have never been drawn to monastic life myself and have never been to Taize, though I still hope to get enough money to go on a pilgrimage to visit the place one day. When I conducted internet research on Brother Roger and the Taize Community, I was struck by the following which I believe is one of the monks' rules: "In living a common life, have we any other end than to unify men who are committed to following Christ and become a living sign of the unity of the Church?" This is then complimented somewhere else by an admirer's comment who says, "It is a lively reassessment of the historical sources and destiny of what followers perceive to be the one, holy, catholic and apostolic church of Jesus Christ." This reminds me of the early Christians; and how I wish the Christian Church of the 21st Century could draw humanity to the Kingdom by putting these ideals into practice!

# Learning to lead for the Kingdom

A Gift to: _____

From: _____

# Endorsements

Few people can claim to be as qualified as Prof Ngara to teach Christians the skills of Gospel-based leadership. Ngara has formed and shaped many leaders of today in his distinguished career as an academic and educator, in his prolific writings, and by his lived example as an activist and a disciple.

For many years it was my privilege to edit a monthly column on Christian leadership written by Prof Ngara. These were presented with clarity, coherence and charity, giving gentle yet firm guidance with profound substance. In those columns, he unpacked complex theological concepts, making accessible knowledge that may otherwise intimidate.

As such, there is no doubt that this book will open the door to Christian leadership to many people, be it in communities or boardrooms, preparing them to help build the Kingdom of God on earth which Christ commands us to. In the perilous times that we live in, prayer is an essential key that authorizes the Lord to step and intervene into believers' affairs in accordance with what is written in their books of destinies.

*Endorsement by Gunther Simmermacher,*
*Editor of The Southern Cross*

# Learning to lead for the Kingdom

As a person that loves leadership and teaches it, I am always fascinated by personalities in the Bible; how they lived, how they led and the legacy they left. It is rare to find leaders that lead well like Jesus Christ. Many books have been written about the leadership of Jesus Christ. Yet not many capture, explain and expound well His life as done by Professor Ngara in this book *LEARNING TO LEAD FOR THE KINGDOM.* He explains in detail, coherently and expertly the leadership style, life and purpose of Our Lord Jesus Christ. Example is the best teacher, and no one learns well except by what they see modelled, promoted and proclaimed: "I have given you an example to follow: do as I have done to you," Jesus Christ said (John 13:15).

It is important to note that Christians of today are Christians because of the obedience of the disciples of Jesus Christ, who after observing Him, having been empowered by the Holy Spirit, went to the then known world with the Gospel… they wanted everyone to know, understand and live in the Kingdom of God. This book challenges today's leaders to think, teach and promote the Kingdom of God as exemplified by Our Lord Jesus Christ and the disciples. I recommend this book to every leader that cares to see the Great Commission accomplished in our life time and generation.

*Dr Phillip Tsvangira:*
*Author, Learn LEAD Legacy: Leadership Lessons from King David*

# TABLE OF CONTENTS

# Learning to lead for the Kingdom

# Foreword

Professor Ngara reflects on leadership for the Kingdom, understanding the meaning of the concept of "Kingdom of God" and the message of Jesus about the Kingdom of God. He raises poignant questions about what was on people's minds in Jesus' time, and the lessons we learn for such a time as this, as the book of Esther states.

The book gives a succinct and practical way to comprehend the narrative of the Kingdom of God when God controls our destinies. It reflects that the sovereignty of God is at work in a particular situation, accomplishing God's purpose without in any way overriding our free will. As such, the book is timely, as it convincingly challenges 21st century Christians to use their free will to cooperate with God in shaping the future of humanity for the better.

Professor Ngara draws upon the remnant motif that recurs throughout the natural disasters, diseases and calamities that threaten God's people throughout the ages. However, as we learn in the book of Esther, the outworking of God's purpose does not eliminate human responsibility for the moral decision and moral action. It is with this view that the book suggests that the Christian Church of the 21st century has the responsibility to examine itself to see how it can best and effectively accomplish the mission given to it by Jesus Christ.

The lenses through which Professor Ngara looks at the Kingdom of God reflects the origins of the Kingdom, the redemption of God's people, and the mission of Jesus through the restoration of God's Kingdom and the salvation of all

i

# Learning to lead for the Kingdom

humanity. He thus reflects on the trajectory of all human history as leading to the reign of Christ, and to the New Heaven and New Earth when Jesus hands over the Kingdom to God the Father "After He has destroyed all dominion, authority and power" (1 Corinthians 15:24). He ably links this with the themes of the origins of the Kingdom, redemption, the second coming of Jesus Christ and the glorious wedding supper of the Lamb prophesied in Chapter 19 of the Book of Revelation.

Professor Ngara firmly holds that God is not absent. Even in the moments when it appears so, he confronts the deepest of our questions and gives us hope for his Kingdom.

While **Learning to Lead for the Kingdom** is addressed to all Christians, it has particular relevance for religious leaders, and for senior students who are being prepared for the leadership of the Church in seminaries, theological colleges, convents and universities.

Read this account and be inspired to lead for the Kingdom of God.


*Most Rev Dr Thabo Makgoba*
*Anglican Archbishop of Cape Town*
*God bless you and increase you in knowledge and understanding of His word, for the edification of the church.*

# INTRODUCTION

## Foregrounding the Kingdom

This book has been written to try and address a number of questions related to Jesus' message on the kingdom of God: First, to ask Christians to think more deeply about the mission of Jesus. The church rightly lays a lot of emphasis on the salvation of humanity as central to the mission of Jesus. Jesus came to save humanity from the sin of Adam and to show all who believe the way to the Father, "For God so loved the world that he gave his one and only Son, that whoever believes in him shall not perish but have eternal life" (John 3:16). But there is a question which many Christians are not clear about: Was Jesus' mission only about salvation for humankind? In his preaching did he only talk about salvation or did he not put emphasis on something else – the kingdom of God? When anyone reads the Bible, how often do they come across these words "the kingdom of God" or "the kingdom of heaven" in Jesus' statements, comments or questions? Is it for nothing that Jesus uses this phrase so frequently? Does the frequency with which the phrase occurs in Jesus' speech not suggest that we pay more attention to its meaning and significance? It is even a key phrase in the only prayer that he taught.

# Learning to lead for the Kingdom

This naturally brings us to the second question: What is the kingdom of God? What do we mean when we pray "Thy kingdom come?" Where is the kingdom supposed to come, and how must it come? And scholars talk a lot about the history of salvation. Can we talk about the salvation of humankind without reference to the kingdom of God? Are the phrases "the kingdom of God" and "the history of salvation" not substantially or even inextricably linked? If they are thus linked, is it proper to put so much stress on the one and not that much on the other? The Kingdom of God is heaven or is in heaven, and God the Father is the King of heaven. Why, then, does Paul, when he talks about the end of the world, say, "Then the end will come, when He hands over the kingdom to God the Father after he has destroyed all dominion, authority and power?" (1 Corinthians 15:24). Which kingdom is Paul referring to here? And why would the Psalmist be inspired to cry out, "The highest heavens belong to the LORD, but the earth He has given to mankind."? (Psalm 115:16). And what "Dominion, authority and power" does Paul say Christ will destroy? Is he not referring to the powers on earth that are opposed to the Kingdom of God in heaven?

The verse which says "Then the end will come, when He hands over the kingdom to God the Father ..." gives a sense of destiny. This is in line with a number of statements made by Jesus Himself; for example, "Then the King will say to those on His right, 'Come, you who are blessed by my Father; take your inheritance, the kingdom prepared for you since the creation of the world" (Matthew 25:34). And "All the nations will be gathered before him..." (Matthew 25:32). There is a sense of destiny here. The world is going somewhere. As Ron Boehme (1989:179) puts it, "The Bible tells us where we have

# Introduction: Foregrounding the Kingdom

come from, God's plan for the present and the future." When Jesus tells Pilate, "My kingdom is not of this world", He is not suggesting that He does not care about the planet earth; He is referring not only to the Kingdom of heaven, but also to this destiny of the earth, "After He has destroyed all dominion, authority and power" that is presently in control of this world. A detailed analysis of the concept of the Kingdom will help the reader to understand precisely this point: Where have human beings come from? Where are they now? And where are we going? This compels the follower of Jesus to go beyond the simple idea that we are born, we live a good or bad life, and then we die and go to heaven or hell, depending on what we have done with our lives, and that is all that is in the future of humankind. It also goes beyond the idea that the planet earth will completely disappear with doomsday. The end will indeed come, and then what? Clarity about this point will help the world to see that Christianity gives hope to a hopeless world, and that our view of the future of the universe is more positive and logical than the idea of "doomsday" as the end of life and of everything we love on planet earth.

With this we come to the fourth issue: How do you lead people to the kingdom? In other words, how do you teach about the kingdom of God? There is fortunately, a growing literature about Jesus' leadership. This includes Ron Boehme's *Leadership for the 21st Century* (1989), C. Gene Wilkes' *Jesus on Leadership* (1998), and Boyd Bailey's *Learning to Lead Like Jesus* (2018), among a host of other books. Among these, it is Ron Boehme's book that attempts to emphasize both Jesus' approach to leadership and the concept of the kingdom of God. When it comes to the theme of the kingdom of God, Ron Boehme must be counted among the pioneering writers on the theme. Among the publications that have foregrounded the theme of the kingdom even more clearly must be counted Albert Nolan's *Jesus Before Christianity* (1992), Myles Munroe's *Kingdom Principles* (2006) and his *Discovering the Kingdom* (2010), as well as John Eldredge's *All Things New* (2017). Reference to these works is not necessarily an indication this author agrees with all the approaches and positions taken in the books and statements made by the authors, but an acknowledgement of the important contribution they have made to the debate on the kingdom of God.

The approach adopted in this book is first to try and bring the reader to a clearer understanding of the concept of the kingdom of God by tracing the development of the kingdom from the very beginning when God created the world, through the present stage after the first coming of Christ, to the second coming of Jesus and the end of the world, and what follows after the end of the world. In this way, the destiny of humankind is explained from the origins of creation to the new creation after the end of the world; and biblically from Genesis to Revelation. Within that structure, the mission of Jesus, His vision of the Kingdom, His approach to leadership and His message to His followers are adumbrated, and hopefully made clearer. It then becomes necessary to show what the role of the followers of Jesus is in proclaiming the kingdom of God, what the challenges of the age are, and how we should prepare ourselves for the task. Preparing ourselves in part includes understanding Jesus' approach to leadership and being aware of how God calls leaders and how we should respond.

This leads to the need to address some of the key issues facing the Christian faith in our time. Some writers see the

# Introduction: Foregrounding the Kingdom

church making great strides, and to some this shows the inroads the kingdom of God is making in our time. Some, perhaps many authors, identify the kingdom of God with the Christian church. Some authorities also identify the New Jerusalem of the Book of Revelation with the Christian church. These are among some of the very important issues that this book seeks to address. Furthermore, in this author's view, the Christian church is facing major challenges in our time, including the real possibility that in this century, for the first time in many centuries, the Christian church will cease to be the largest religion of the world. This and other negative developments present some serious Christians with the challenge of what to do in order to fulfil the commandments given to us by the Lord, and this includes the Great Commission (See Matthew 28:16-20).

The challenges referred to above further entail asking ourselves what kind of Christians we ought to be in the temporal world. Is it enough to regard ourselves as Christians in the general sense of which the term is used today, or should we rather see ourselves as "citizens of the kingdom" who are *in* this world, but not *of* this world? And if that is the case, how should we relate to the world? What is it that will make these "citizens of the kingdom" different from those who are not members of this citizenship; or do we think it does not matter at all that we are seen to have some distinguishing characteristics? To put it differently, what is it that we should do to ensure the church makes an effective impact on the world as we go forward? Is going to church on Sunday sufficient as a sign that shows we are genuine disciples of Jesus?

# Learning to lead for the Kingdom

On my part as a baptized Christian, a Bible scholar and a disciple of Jesus burning with the desire to see the Lord's mission propagated in the world as He would want to see it done, I am deeply concerned to know there are so many billions of people in the world who know either very little or nothing about Jesus; and that billions more who in percentage figures constitute as much as 50% of the number of believing Christians, have turned their backs on Jesus Christ and other religions and fall under the ever growing category of secularism. This, to me, is one of the major challenges facing the church today. "I have come to bring fire on the earth," Jesus once said, "And how I wish it were already kindled!" (Luke 12:49). I have said to myself, the early Christians did indeed kindle the fire and set it blazing. Can we, in the face of all these factors, honestly claim that the fire is still blazing in our time? I, for one, am not convinced we have sufficient justification to make that claim.

Together with my recently departed wife, Bernice Teboho Ngara, I have taught the subject of Christian Leadership to pastors and religious leaders from different denominations, and have taught students training for the ministry. I could have written a book related to those experiences and the subject that we taught. Some of the chapters of this book are informed by that experience. However, there are writings that are inspired by the Holy Spirit who distributes His gifts to anyone of us "Just as He determines" (1 Corinthians 12:11). This means that even to humble teachers like myself with no position in the church, "The manifestation of the Spirit is given for the common good" (1 Corinthians 12:7). I believe this is the case with this book which I have written in response to what I believe is the call of the Lord, and is based on a thorough study

# Introduction: Foregrounding the Kingdom

of the Bible. To this end, I am grateful to learn from the writings of more enlightened scholars, be they Evangelicals, Reformists, Anglicans, Catholics, Orthodox or Pentecostals.

This view comes from the deep conviction that Jesus Christ, Our Lord and Saviour, is burning with the desire to see His followers obeying His commands and demonstrating the love to each other that He has shown to them and to the rest of humanity. "If you love me, keep my commands." And "Whoever has my commands and keeps them is the one who loves me." (John 14:15, 21). And what is one of the main key of His commands? It is surely this: "A new command I give you: Love one another. As I have loved you, so you must love one another. By this everyone will know that you are my disciples, if you love one another." (John 13:34-35). To me, whatever differences we may have, should not be seen to be greater than this command. Theological, doctrinal, and ecclesial differences are real and can neither be ignored nor swept under the carpet. It will certainly take time to come to an agreement on these issues. But does this mean we should not obey the command to love one another?

Referring to the title of his book *UnChristian,* David Kinnaman (Kinnaman 2007:15) has made this comment: "In fact, the title of this book, *unChristian,* reflects outsiders' most common reaction to the faith: they think Christianity no longer represents what Jesus had in mind, that Christianity in our society is not what it was meant to be." Kinnaman is referring to American society here, but what he says applies to most Christian societies. As he points out on page 35 of the same book: "The church desperately needs more people who facilitate a deeper, more authentic vision of the Christian faith

# Learning to lead for the Kingdom

in our pluralistic, sophisticated culture". Josh McDowell presents a somewhat different but equally compelling view about the need to present an authentic view of Christianity to young people. He suggests the first task of adult Christians in their effort to teach young people about the truth of Christianity is to become "Living models" of it in our very lives: "No message will sink in faster or take root deeper than the one that is demonstrated by the nature of our lives" ( McDowell & Bellis 2006:68). Christian love and unity are part of that deeper and more authentic vision of the Christian faith referred to by Kinnaman, and demonstrating them in relations between Christians of different denominations is an important part of becoming "Living models" of our faith.

This book is not just about young people, nor is it only about America as is the case with Kinnaman and McDowell. It has a broader audience - that should be clear by now. The issue of demonstrating Christian love and unity just referred to above is seen as one that should be of concern to all who care about Jesus' commands to His followers, and about the role of Christians and the church in the modern world. It is appropriate to ask the question: Should differences in theology impede ecumenical activities? Some progress has indeed been made since the rise of ecumenism in the 20th century, but for us lay Christians there is not much evidence of the progress that is being made to change the age old negative attitudes towards one another.

The view just expressed above reminds me of Jesus' instructions to his disciples who tried to stop someone who was driving out demons in the Lord's name when he was not one of the Lord's disciples. "Do not stop him," Jesus said, "For

# Introduction: Foregrounding the Kingdom

whoever is not against you, is for you." (Luke 9:49-50). If the Lord Himself could give credit to people who used His name even when they were not His disciples, why should we not tolerate those who spread the gospel message of Jesus with a sincere heart even if they belong to a different church? I say this cognisant of the fact that there are many sects today which seem to use the gospel of Jesus for reasons other than spiritual. I have very strong reservations about such groups. For instance, I am suspicious of the so-called health and wealth groups of churches. I still need to be convinced that some of the leaders of such organisations have not set up the churches in order to enrich themselves. For me this is so different from the leaders of the 16th century Reformation who were genuinely concerned about what they thought was the extent to which the church was departing from the Scriptures. Martin Luther's aim, for example, was not to set up a church, but to correct what he thought was wrong in the church.

The last five hundred years since the Reformation in what was called the "Western church", the battle between churches has largely been a battle of ideas: What is the correct interpretation of the Bible? Which church or group of churches is fulfilling the requirements of the Bible? Which is the true church of Christ? etc. While there are still raging debates on these and similar issues, new challenges are now beginning to emerge. I begin by quoting two authorities: Myles Munroe (2010:109) states, "Jesus came to earth, not to bring a religion, but a Kingdom – the governing influence of the Kingdom of heaven on earth." On his part Ron Boehme (1989) says, "The Bible never encourages us to preach the Church, because that would easily become focused on self and self-serving. We are told to *build* the Church and *preach* the

# Learning to lead for the Kingdom

Kingdom." The focus should therefore be on the *Kingdom* and not on the *denomination*. The new questions that arise in our time therefore, include the following: Should we spend all our time talking about how wrong the other churches are, or should we not rather seek ways to correct each other in a spirit of mercy and love? Will Christianity survive in the face of competing religions and ideologies? How can we fulfil the Lord's command to preach the gospel to all nations and all creation? If Christianity survives, what kind of Christians ought we to be? And, divided though we are, how can we work together to obey the Lord's commands and to achieve the mission for which Jesus built the church?

Before coming to the conclusion of this introduction, it is necessary for me to explain that while the book is addressed to church leaders and others in positions of influenced in the church, part of my intention as an author is that the book be used as a resource for academics and the training of senior students in the subject of "Kingdom Studies". I strongly believe that students who are being trained for ministry should be exposed to at least one course in Kingdom Studies. In that regard, this book can be used as a key text for such a course. What I have tried to do, is to separate the material for training students from the main text of the book. Consequently, the section on training is added in the form of appendices to the book. Those who want to use the book without having to refer to the study section can do so; and those who wish to use it as a textbook or as an aid to Kingdom Studies can refer to the relevant section of the book.

The book is therefore divided into two main parts and an Appendices section. Part I is about the kingdom of God and

# Introduction: Foregrounding the Kingdom

the mission of Jesus, including His teachings on Leadership. Part II is about how we, Jesus' followers in the 21ˢᵗ century, should carry out the mission He has given to us, and this includes training in how God calls people to leadership and how we should respond to His call. Then, Part III consists of two appendices on Kingdom Studies.

Finally, I thank the Lord for drawing my attention to the works of the authors who have assisted me in my endeavour to try and clarify the importance of Jesus' message on the kingdom of God; and I hope this book will play its role in inspiring fellow believers to regard themselves as citizens of the kingdom dedicated to spreading the Kingdom of God on earth.

# Part I:

# UNDERSTANDING THE KINGDOM AND JESUS'MISSION

# CHAPTER ONE

## The Concept of the Kingdom Of God

God created the earth and put all creatures we know on it – animals, fish, birds – all things that move on land, on the earth and under the earth, in rivers and seas. He then created humankind in His own image and gave them the responsibility to be in charge of all His creation on earth (Genesis 1:26-28). He put the man and woman He had created in the Garden of Eden (Genesis 2:7-8).

Myles Munroe (2006) uses the concept of "Colonization" to explain what God did here. God colonized the earth by sending humankind to govern the planet for him. Adam and Eve were therefore given leadership responsibilities, and the human race was created to be a race of rulers governing and managing the earth on God's behalf. As ruler of heaven, God had created a perfect world which His representative would manage on His behalf. The earth was God's kingdom away from heaven, giving glory to God under the leadership of humankind.

But first, what is a kingdom? A kingdom is a system of governing headed by a king. This system of governing is different from that of a republic, a dictatorship or socialism. A

1

republic, such as South Africa, the United States of America or Ireland (the Republic of Ireland), is led by a president. In today's world, there are kingdoms such as the United Kingdom of Great Britain and Northern Ireland or the Kingdom of Lesotho that have a constitutional queen or king who is a ceremonial head, while the actual governing system is in the hands of a democratically elected government headed by a prime minister. Albert Nolan (1992: 83, 84) says the Greek word *basileia* which has been translated in English as "kingdom" means "kingship" or "royal power". So, God's Kingdom is God's *basileia* or God's political power. On his part, Myles Munroe (2006: 42) argues that the kingdom concept was God's idea, hence, simply stated, "The Bible is about a King, a Kingdom and a royal family of children." In this book, in agreement with Munroe, we shall refer to people who believe in the Bible and are genuine followers of Jesus as the "citizens of the kingdom". This leads to the question "Where is the kingdom of God?"

## *Realms of the Kingdom of God*

The Scriptures seem to refer to three realms that may help in answering this question: Heaven, hell and the earth. These are physical places, meaning that heaven and hell are as real as our planet earth. Heaven is where God and His angels and saints are (although God is everywhere), where Jesus came from and where He returned to at the time of His ascension. It seems to be the place where Abraham and Lazarus were when the rich man saw them in the parable (Luke 16:19-31). This is the place where members of religions such as Christianity, Islam and Judaism want to go when they die. This

# The Concept of the Kingdom of God

surely is the place about which Jesus said, "My Father's house has many rooms" (John 14:2). This, therefore, is where the Kingdom of God is, which is why the "Kingdom of God" is also referred to as "The kingdom of heaven" as is evident in many of Jesus' statements. When we die, our bodies go back to dust until the last day, but the souls of the elect go to heaven, to the Kingdom of God in heaven, where Jesus has prepared a place for them (John 14:2-30). This book is not about this realm. As an author I do not believe I have been given the knowledge and authority to write about heaven. All I can say is heaven is real; it is not a fairy tale, as many of us seem to think. Anyone who wants to know more about heaven, or has doubts about it being real, is invited to read Choo Thomas' book, *Heaven Is So Real!*, published in the USA by Charisma House and in South Africa by Struik Christian Media. Reading that book will bring to life what Paul says to the Corinthians: "What no eye has seen, what no ear has heard, and what no human mind has conceived – the things God has prepared for those who love him…" (1 Corinthians 2:9).

The second realm is hell which Jesus refers to in some of his sayings and is also referred to in Revelation (e.g. Revelation 20:14-15). This surely is the place where the rich man was in the parable mentioned above. This is a place of torture and torment, according to Christian tradition. We do not have much more to say about this realm in this book, except to point out that hell is real and is clearly not part of God's kingdom.

Our focus in this book will be on planet earth, which I have already referred to as "God's kingdom away from heaven". This is the third of the three realms referred to above. As the Psalmist says, "The highest heavens belong to the

3

LORD, but the earth He has given to mankind." (Psalm 115:16). In this regard, the Kingdom of God on earth can be seen as an extension of God's Kingdom in heaven. Using Myles Munroe's concept of colonization and taking the example of a country like, say, Kenya, during colonial times, we can say the Government of Kenya then was not a separate independent government, but an extension of the Government of the United Kingdom in London, as all important decisions about Kenya were taken in London. Government officials in Kenya were representatives of the British Government. I give this example not to justify colonialism, but to give an analogy of the relationship between Paradise and the kingdom of God in heaven. The point at issue is that Adam and Eve in Paradise were representatives of God's Kingdom in heaven. We focus on this realm with a view to clarifying Jesus' teaching about the kingdom of God. In discussing Jesus' teaching we shall divide "God's earthly Kingdom" into three phases: first, the original kingdom established by God under the rulership of Adam and Eve; second, the Kingdom of God during the time of the redemption of human beings by the Son of God, meaning the whole time since Jesus came and died for us until the end of the world; and the third shall be the Reign of Christ on earth when Christ shall reign the world with his saints for one thousand years (See Revelation 20) after what scholars have referred to as "The great catastrophe" (Nolan 1992:61), or "The tribulation" (e.g. Hindson & Hitchcock 2017). At this period Satan will be in prison in the Abyss. After the thousand years he will be released for a short time, and will deceive the nations again before he is thrown into the lake of burning fire. Eternity will then follow when there is a new heaven and a new earth. This is the fourth and final phase, when there is what

# The Concept of the Kingdom of God

John Eldredge (2017) has called "The marriage of heaven and earth". It is necessary for me to clarify that while I use Eldredge's terminology here, my interpretation is different from his as he fuses the third and final phases into one.

We shall refer to the time of Adam and Eve as the Original Kingdom or the First Phase of the Kingdom of God on earth; the time of redemption, namely, including our time, as the Second Phase of the Kingdom; and the thousand years before Eternity as the Third Phase. The present earth has existed since the creation of the world and is the same earth on which Adam and Eve lived; while the future earth will come into being at the time of Jesus' second coming. We begin with an account of the First Phase.

### God's Original Kingdom on Earth

The first phase of the kingdom has been extensively written about by Myles Munroe (Munroe 2006 & 2010). In this chapter we make a very brief account that humankind was created to rule on behalf of God and this fact is clear from the following passages:

'Then God said, "Let us make mankind in our image, in our likeness, so that they may rule over the fish in the sea and the birds in the sky, over the livestock and all the wild animals, and over all the creatures that move along the ground." So God created mankind in His own image, in the image of God He created them; male and female He created them.' (Genesis 1:26-27).

'God blessed them and said to them, "Be fruitful and increase in number; fill the earth and subdue it. Rule over the fish in the sea and the birds in the sky and over every living creature that moves on the ground'" (Genesis 1:28).

We note here that humankind was to rule over all living things: fish, birds, livestock, wild animals and over every living thing. If humankind was to rule over all living creatures, no living creature could harm humanity. Furthermore, humankind was placed in the Garden of Eden and was "To work it and take care of it" (See Genesis 2:8-17). There is no indication at this stage that humans were to rule over other human beings. We are further told that God gave Adam the authority to give names to all animals and birds: "… and whatever the man called each living creature, that was its name. So the man gave names to all the livestock, the birds in the sky and all the wild animals" (Genesis 2:19-20). The power to give names to other creatures is an indication of the authority God had given to humankind to rule the earth on His behalf. It was delegated authority. All created things on earth were to give glory to God under the rulership of humankind. God, the King of heaven, had given humanity a beautiful kingdom to rule on His behalf. This kingdom was an external part of the Kingdom of heaven, meaning that it was an extension of God's heavenly Kingdom. As an extension of the Kingdom of heaven, the earth must have been an idyllic, utopian planet where everything was pleasant and human beings were meant to live in happiness, contentment, without any fear or anxiety. The Psalmist aptly proclaimed, "The highest heavens belong to the LORD, but the earth he has given to humankind" (Psalm 115:16). What a privilege, and what a great honour for humanity!

### The Fall and its Aftermath

*The Testing of God's Chosen Leaders*

# The Concept of the Kingdom of God

However, God often tests the key leaders, if not every leader He appoints. Thus Abraham was tested, Jesus was tested and Adam himself was tested. In all these cases, the test is a test of obedience. Does the appointee obey God? We know that Abraham obeyed God when he was first told to leave his own country (See Genesis 12: 1-5). But a much harder test was to come, and this is the test that really determined whether Abraham was obedient to God or not, for in this test God did not only not promise any reward, but asked Abraham to do something that was most difficult to do for any parent – to sacrifice the son he had so dearly and passionately yearned to have (See Genesis 15: 2-3; 22:1-11).

Jesus was tempted by the devil and proved His loyalty to God (See Matthew 4:1-11). He was loyal to his Father to the extent of accepting death (See Matthew 26: 39, 42; Luke 22:42). Not only did He accept death, but was obedient to the extent of subjecting Himself to the most despicable form of dying, a form that was reserved for slaves and the lowest of human beings, namely, death on a cross! (See Philippians 2:8).

## The Kingdom Lost to Humankind – Adam's Test

God planted a garden in Eden. In the middle of the garden were two trees – the tree of life and the tree of the knowledge of good and evil. This was Adam's test: not to eat from the tree of the knowledge of good and evil (See Genesis 2:16-17). Compare this test with the tests given to Abraham and Jesus. Nevertheless Adam disobeyed God and ate of the fruit just as his wife had done (Genesis 3: 6-7). This act of disobedience had enormous consequences – it upset the whole system that God had put in place on planet earth. Because of the enormity

of their sin, Adam and Eve were banished from the Garden of
Eden where they had lived in God's earthly Kingdom as his
representatives, ruling and managing His creation on His
behalf. They had betrayed God's trust in them and could no
longer be His representative. Now suffering and death became
the lot of human beings (See Genesis 3:17-19). Satan, the devil,
who had been defeated in heaven by God's loyal angels had
now entered the world and taken over the kingdom that had
been given to humankind (See Revelation 12:7-9).

By sinning against God, we lost the earthly kingdom to
Satan. Myles Munroe (2006:41) puts it this way: "The Fall of
man was not the loss of heaven but rather the loss of the
Kingdom government of heaven on earth." The Lord had
given this planet to us to manage and rule on his behalf, but
this authority and its glory came to naught when Adam and
Eve disobeyed God. By listening to and obeying the deceitful
words of Satan, we handed the kingdom over to him. But God
did not abandon us; He still loved and cared for the man and
woman who had sinned against Him. He even helped to cover
their nakedness: "The LORD God made garments of skin for
Adam and his wife and clothed them" (Genesis 3:21). Here we
may see the mercy of God which is explained in the Parable of
the Lost Son (See Luke 15:11-32).

### The Perpetual Struggle between Good and Evil

With Satan's entry in the world, the perpetual struggle
between Good and Evil began. Evil began to dominate. The
earth which God had created as His Kingdom away from
heaven, as an extension of the Kingdom of Heaven, was now
under the control of Satan and no longer reflected the values

# The Concept of the Kingdom of God

of heaven. The first recorded major indication of the victory of Evil over Good after the *fall* was the sin of murder in the first degree – the murder of Abel by his brother Cain. What this also shows is that the sins of jealousy, hatred and anger were beginning to show their ugly faces. The Lord had even warned Cain, "But if you do not do what is right, sin is crouching at your door; it desires to have you, but you must rule over it." (See Genesis 4:6-7). But sin ruled over Cain and he killed his brother. From then on, wickedness began to spread rapidly in the world, so much so that "The LORD regretted that he had made human beings on the earth, and His heart was deeply troubled" (Genesis 6:6). Because of this the Lord brought the flood with a view to wipe from the face of the earth the human beings He had made together with the animals, birds and other creatures that He had given to Adam and Eve to rule over. How happy the devil must have been to see his rebellion against heaven permeating the whole earth!

The ongoing battle between Good and Evil is played out in Revelation, the only book of the New Testament that is dedicated to prophecy. In Chapter 11 we are informed that Good will triumph over Evil in this world: "The kingdom of the world has become the kingdom of our Lord and His Messiah, and He will reign for ever and ever" (Revelation 11: 13). This verse should help us understand better what Jesus says about the coming of His reign at the end of the world: "Then the King will say to those on His right, 'Come, you who are blessed by my Father; take your inheritance, the Kingdom prepared for you since the creation of the world'"(Matthew 25:34). Surely this is a reference to the original Kingdom of God on earth which we lost when Adam and Eve disobeyed God and were thrown out of Paradise?

9

# Learning to lead for the Kingdom

Through Adam and Eve's disobedience we lost what Paul refers to as our "Sonship" (See Galatians 4:1-7; Romans 8:14-17) and regained it when Christ redeemed us. This is the inheritance that Peter says is kept in heaven for those of us who "Through faith are shielded by God's power until the coming of the salvation that is ready to be revealed in the last time" (1 Peter 1:4-5). The battle between Good and Evil is about the kingdom we lost to Satan. In Chapter 12 of Revelation the battle between the good angels led by Michael and the devil and his angels is portrayed, as well as the fury of the devil against the woman who gave birth to Jesus (See Revelation 12:1-17). The woman surely stands for Mary, the mother of Jesus, although some readers will think the woman symbolises Israel, the nation through whom the Messiah came into the world. Satan is finally "Thrown into the lake of burning sulphur" (Revelation 20:10).

## The Plan for the Restoration of the Kingdom

God loved the human beings He had made, and He wanted to restore the Kingdom that Adam and Eve had lost to the devil. The time of Noah going back to the banishment of Adam and Eve from Eden can be regarded as a dark period, or a pre-Covenant period when God had not yet put in place the plan leading to the restoration of the Kingdom. In order to restore His Kingdom on earth, God first called Abraham to establish the race of the Chosen People. On calling Abram, the Lord had said, "and all peoples on earth will be blessed through you" (Genesis 12: 3). As part of the process of moulding the Chosen People and restoring the Kingdom, God gave the Law to Moses. A key feature of the Law was the Ten

10

# The Concept of the Kingdom of God

Commandments (See Exodus 20:1-17; Deuteronomy 5:6-21). But God did not just give the Law to Moses. He also told Moses about the coming of the Messiah when He said, "I will raise up for them a prophet like you from among their fellow Israelites, and I will put my words in his mouth. He will tell them everything I command him." (Deuteronomy 18:15, 18). This prophet was more than a prophet for he would save humanity from the sin of Adam. The Israelites were supposed to listen to him. This may be purely coincidental, but the words of Moses to the Israelites echo what the Lord said at the time of the transfiguration: "You must listen to him" (Deuteronomy 18:15), and "Listen to him!" (Matthew 17:5).

From time to time, throughout the Old Testament, God called prophets to remind the Israelites of God's ways and to warn them against their waywardness and disobedience. Some of the prophets, such as Isaiah, prophesied about the coming of the Messiah, the Saviour. The last of these prophets was John the Baptist who prepared the way of the Lord as had been prophesied by Isaiah. This takes us to Jesus and his mission.

# Learning to lead for the Kingdom

# CHAPTER TWO

❧

# The Restoration of the Kingdom
# Jesus and His Mission

## *Jesus Announces His Mission*

John preached the baptism of repentance and made it clear he was not the Messiah (See John 1:19-23). John testified about Jesus. On seeing Jesus he said, "Look, the Lamb of God, who takes away the sin of the world!" (John 1:29). He went on to say, "I have seen and testify that this is God's Chosen One" (John 1:34). Later on John testified again about Jesus, "I am not the Messiah but am sent ahead of Him" (John 3:28). It should be remembered that the birth of John and the birth of Jesus were both announced by the Angel Gabriel who went to Mary six months after he had announced the birth of John (See Luke 1: 11-38).

What then, was Jesus' mission? What was His message? What did He say about the primary purpose of His coming into the world? Did He come primarily for the purpose of establishing the Christian church, or was there something more fundamental than the church? It is interesting to note that Jesus went to Nazareth where He was brought up to announce His mission. He went into the synagogue as was His custom. He stood up to read, and the scroll of the prophet Isaiah was handed to him. He unrolled it and found the passage He wanted to read, and He read:

"The Spirit of the Lord is on me because He has anointed Me to proclaim good news to the poor. He sent me to proclaim freedom for the prisoners and recovery of sight for the blind, to set the oppressed free, to proclaim the year of the Lord's favour" (Isaiah 6: 1-2). 'He then said, "Today this scripture is fulfilled in your hearing"' (Luke 4: 16-21).

On this particular day He was first admired by his listeners who ended up rejecting Him. The sequence of events preceding and following this event is not clear, but what seems clear is that after the temptation in the desert following His baptism by John, and after John had been put in prison, Jesus withdrew to Galilee. From that time onwards Jesus was preoccupied with the following: preaching and teaching about the Kingdom of God, calling His disciples (done over a short period of time), healing the sick, opening the eyes of the blind, driving out evil spirits and forgiving sins. Doing this was an important part of Jesus' mission.

### The Dual Nature of Jesus' Mission

Myles Munroe (2006:20) has suggested few ordained ministers and priests of the Christian Church have been trained in kingdom studies: "Their priority is in propagating the Christian religion rather than the message and concepts of the Kingdom of God." If this is true, there is a major gap that needs to be filled in the training of Christian ministers and priests, considering the importance of the concept of "the

# The Restoration of the Kingdom - Jesus and His Mission

kingdom of God" or "kingdom of heaven" in the New Testament. For example, each of the three synoptic gospels says something about the priority that Jesus put on preaching and teaching about the kingdom of God at the beginning of His public ministry. I quote from each evangelist:

Matthew: *From that time on Jesus began to preach, "Repent, for the Kingdom of heaven has come near"* (Matthew 4:17).

Mark: *"The time has come,"* he said. *"The Kingdom of God has come near. Repent and believe the good news!"* (Mark 1:14).

Luke: *But he said, "I must proclaim the good news of the kingdom of God to the other towns also, because that is why I was sent"* (Luke 4:43).

John does not quote Jesus making this kind of pronouncement at the beginning of his ministry, but it is from John that we hear Jesus making some very important statements about the Kingdom. For our purposes here, I shall quote two statements Jesus made in the context of His discussion with the Samaritan woman at the well. When the disciples who had gone into the town to buy food returned, they urged Him to eat and they were surprised by His response. First he said, *"I have food to eat that you know nothing about."* The evangelist then goes on to quote Him elaborating on this bewildering statement: *"My food",* said Jesus, *"is to do the will of him who sent me and to finish his work"* (John 4: 31-34). These two statements show just how committed Jesus was to His mission. As I pointed out in an earlier publication (Ngara 2004:56), "So central was this mission to His life that it was this that sustained Him in the same way that food sustains life in ordinary human

15

beings". The concept of the Kingdom of God (or the Kingdom of heaven) is at the very heart of Jesus' mission.

Going hand in hand with the concept of "The Kingdom of God" is the word "Repent". Repentance means turning away from sin; it entails not only being sorry for the sins one has committed, but becoming transformed so that one is a new person. This is one of the key issues in Jesus' discussion with Nicodemus in Chapter 3 of John's Gospel (John 3:1-15): "Very truly, I tell you, no one can see the Kingdom of God unless they are born again." Consequently, being born again is the condition for entering the kingdom of God. Being born again entails this kind of repentance that leads to the spiritual creation of a new person. Having been born in flesh by our mothers, we must be born again of the Spirit. Hence, "Flesh gives birth to flesh, but the Spirit gives birth to spirit." We must be born again of water and the Spirit – hence, the importance of the Sacrament of Baptism in the Christian tradition. As Paul says, "Your whole self-ruled by the flesh was put off when you were circumcised by Christ having been buried with him in baptism" (Colossians 2:11-12). And again, "Therefore, if anyone is in Christ, the new creation has come. The old has gone, the new is here!" (1 Corinthians 5:17).

The discussion between Jesus and Nicodemus points to another important aspect of Jesus' mission: "Just as Moses lifted up the snake in the wilderness, so the Son of Man must be lifted up, that everyone who believes may have eternal life in him." And the evangelist goes on to say, "For God so loved the world that he gave his one and only Son, that whoever believes in him shall not perish but have eternal life" (John 3: 14-16). This points to Jesus' mission of salvation which has

# The Restoration of the Kingdom - Jesus and His Mission

been so clearly understood and emphasized by the Christian church. This aspect of Jesus' mission is what John emphasises at the beginning of his Gospel. Thus in the very first chapter he points out: "Yet to all who did receive him, to those who believed in his name, he gave the right to become children of God – children born not of natural descent, nor of human decision or a husband's will, but born of God" (John 1:12-13). Being born again therefore, means being born of God through the Spirit. This is what Paul describes as our "Adoption to sonship". It is by being born again through the Spirit that we are now entitled to call God *"Abba,* Father," because now we are heirs of God and co-heirs with Christ" (See Romans 8:14-17).

At this juncture, we are now in a position to answer the question "What was Jesus' mission?" The answer then becomes clear: Jesus' mission had two dimensions to it: First, to proclaim the Kingdom of God, to announce the coming of the Kingdom; and second, to save humanity from the sin of Adam and Eve. These two dimensions are inseparably linked to one another. By sinning against God we lost the kingdom to Satan; but not only did we lose the kingdom, we also lost the right to "Sonship" – hence our parents were driven out of the Garden of Eden where they had enjoyed a close relationship and fellowship with God. Outside Eden we were in a world that was now dominated by the evil one and where we lost our original relationship with God as well as our inheritance. Henceforth, humanity was forever searching for the way back to the Kingdom and to our inheritance, developing unenlightened routes to God in the form of various beliefs and religions; and setting up political and governance systems that some thought would lead to human happiness, such as socialism, Marxism-Leninism and democracy.

## Jesus as the Innocent Lamb of God

To show us our way back to the Kingdom, God had to send His one and only Son to become one of us and to show what it means to be a child of God and a citizen of the Kingdom of God. But it was not enough for Him to come and show us the way: Our rebellion against God had been of such a magnitude, was so enormous and so treacherous, we could not be simply restored to our original relationship with God by just knowing the way to the Father. Someone had to buy our inheritance back with his own life. But this could not be done by any human being who had faults and was sinful like Adam. In the Jewish tradition, the Passover Lamb that was sacrificed had to be a perfect lamb without any blemish. Joe Amaral (2011:130 ff) explains that for the Passover Feast, the High Priest would go to Bethlehem to find a perfect lamb. This lamb would be examined before its slaughter to confirm that it was without blemish. Amaral says Matthew, who was Jewish writing for a Jewish audience, is the only evangelist who includes the incident of Pilate washing his hands to signify that he found Jesus innocent (See Matthew 27:24).

Significantly, Amaral observes that by washing his hands and saying, "I am innocent of this man's blood," Pilate was unknowingly echoing the Jewish tradition of atonement for an unsolved murder when the elders of the town were supposed to wash their hands and say, "Our hands did not shed this blood, nor did our eyes see it done." I would further add that significantly also, the elders would go on to say, "Accept this atonement for your people Israel, whom You have redeemed,

# The Restoration of the Kingdom - Jesus and His Mission

LORD, and do not hold your people guilty of the blood of an innocent person" (Deuteronomy 21:8-7). In the case of Jesus, contrary to this act of atonement, 'All the people answered, "His blood is on us and on our children"' (Matthew 27:25). Thus Pilate unknowingly confirmed the testimony of John the Baptist who, on seeing Jesus, said, "Look, the Lamb of God, who takes away the sin of the world" (John 1:29). And taken together John's testimony and Jesus' conduct before Pilate when He gave no answer to the false charges made against Him (Matthew 27:12-14) resonated with the prophecy of Isaiah: "He was oppressed and afflicted, yet He did not open His mouth; He was led like a Lamb to the slaughter, and as a sheep before its shearers is silent, so He did not open His mouth" (Isaiah 53: 7).

The discussion we have had here should lead us to conclude that it was only Jesus who was fit to restore our lost Kingdom and our inheritance as children of God. Writing about what God has done for us through Jesus, the God who became human, C.S. Lewis suggests that what Christ did for us which we could not do ourselves as the whole human race is this "That the business of becoming a son of God, of being turned from being a created thing into a begotten thing, of passing over from the temporary biological life into timeless 'spiritual' life, has been done for us" (C.S.Lewis:2012:181). The basic work of salvation has been done for us by God's Son, whose Father we rebelled against. The channel of being born again has been opened for us! What we need to do is to repent! Let us rejoice and thank the Lord. We should, however, bear in mind that it is not enough to focus only on being born again and joyfully crying out "We are saved! We are saved!" Being

19

born again is the first step in our growth as citizens of the Kingdom. There is another equally important obligation – to play our role in building the kingdom of God on earth!

To complete our characterisation of Jesus as our Redeemer we need to get answers to several other questions: First, was He the Prophet that God told Moses He would raise among the Israelites? Was He the Messiah the prophets spoke about? Was He the Emmanuel prophesied by Isaiah (Isaiah 7:14)? Was He the Prince of Peace and Wonderful Counsellor who was to reign on David's throne (Isaiah 9: 6-7)? Was He the shoot that was to come up from the stump of Jesse on whom the Spirit of the Lord would rest and who would judge with righteousness and justice? (Isaiah 11:1-4). The second question is, if He was the Messiah, was He the kind of Messiah that the Jews expected who would come and rule Israel and deliver its people from the oppression of the Romans and other gentile nations? The third question is, what was Jesus' vision of the Kingdom of God?

On the question whether Jesus was the Messiah, the evangelists had no doubt (See Matthew 1:16-18; Luke 2:25-32; John 1:41). From the passage he read in Nazareth and the comment "Today this scripture is fulfilled in your hearing, we can conclude that Jesus Himself, understood Himself to be the Saviour that the prophets had spoken about. He was the prophet that God said He would raise from among the Israelites (See Deuteronomy 18:15- 18). The Israelites had told Moses they did not want God Himself to speak to them directly, or they would die (See Deuteronomy 18:16), and God had said He would raise one among them and further added "I will put my words in his mouth. He will tell them everything I command Him" (Deuteronomy 18:18-19). He then sent His Son in human form whom the Israelites could see because He was not as frightening as the God of Sinai was, but who spoke God's words (See John 5:36-40; John 8:42-43; John 12:4-46; John 14:6; John 14:10, etc). Jesus confirmed He was the Messiah when He endorsed Peter's declaration (See Matthew 16:13-20). Furthermore, we have already quoted passages that prove He was the Messiah. The issue of His birth as prophesied by Isaiah, can be answered from reading Matthew 1:17-25; Luke 1:26-38 and Luke 2:1-7; and from an examination of the vision He had of the kingdom. The question whether He was the kind of Messiah the Jewish leaders expected can be answered from His response to Pilate when He said, "My kingdom is not of this world" (John 18:36) and from His rejection by the Jewish leaders. This takes us to the third question: What was Jesus' vision of the Kingdom of God? Before we can answer this question, we need to explain this: Why does Jesus choose to say, "The Kingdom of God has come near", and not "The kingdom of God *is here*"? We attempt to answer this question in the next section of this chapter.

## The Second Phase of the Kingdom

*Distinguishing between the Second, Third and Final Phases of the Kingdom*

In the previous chapter, we made a distinction between the Second Phase of the Kingdom and the Third Phase. This distinction is merely for the purpose of making us humans understand better how the Kingdom of God on earth has unfolded. There is a difference between the Kingdom of God in the world as we know it today, and the Kingdom of God Jesus refers to when He tells His disciples, "Truly, I tell you, I will not drink again from the fruit of the vine until that day when I drink it new in the kingdom of God" (Mark 14:25). The new wine is not the wine we drink in this temporal and fallen world; it is the wine we shall drink with Christ when His reign has been revealed. It is the wine we shall drink at that feast about which Jesus says, "People will come from east and west and north and south, and will take their places at the feast in the kingdom of God" (Luke 13:29).

There is the Kingdom of God in the here and now, when Jesus tells the Pharisees, "The Kingdom of God is in your midst" (Luke 17:21), and the Kingdom of God Jesus refers to when He tells His disciples, "At that time they will see the Son of Man coming in a cloud with power and great glory… Even so, when you see these things happening, you know that the Kingdom of God is near" (Luke 21:27-31). This Kingdom of God that Jesus refers to here, is the time of the One Thousand Years when he will be ruling the world as king with His saints, and when Satan is in prison in the Abyss (See Revelation 20:1-6). Following this will be Eternity (See Revelation 21 & 22) "When He hands over the Kingdom to God the Father after He has destroyed all dominion, authority and power" (1 Corinthians 15:24). The division of the Kingdom into these phases should lead to a better understanding of statements like, "And surely I will be with you always, to the very end of the age." The end of the age here, surely does not refer to the end of the apostolic era or the end of Roman colonization. Jesus must have been referring to the end of the second phase of the

# The Restoration of the Kingdom - Jesus and His Mission

kingdom, before His second coming. We need to elaborate more on the second and third phases of the Kingdom, as well as on the fourth and eternal phase that we call Eternity.

That Jesus referred to the Kingdom of God in the here and now can be gleaned from the following: "The Kingdom of God has come near" and from the statement "Thy Kingdom come" in the Lord's Prayer. The Kingdom of God is not yet fully here with us. It has come close to us and God is no longer as distant as He was after the Fall because He has sent his one and only Son to live among us, to be one of us and to show us the way back to the Father by re-introducing the values of the Kingdom we lost when we were thrown out of Eden.

When we say "Thy kingdom come" in the Lord's Prayer, we are asking God to help us demonstrate we are "The people of God," that we are indeed "Citizens of the kingdom." I would therefore, argue that in the Lord's Prayer we are asking for God's Kingdom to come in two ways: First, we are asking for the actual Kingdom of God, the Reign of Christ, to come, namely, the true and real Kingdom of God when Christ is ruling this world, and the values of God and heaven, are the dominant values of humanity. Second, we are asking for the manifestation of the Kingdom of God in *our present world* – in this second phase of the Kingdom. That manifestation takes the form that Jesus demonstrated: Freedom for the oppressed and downtrodden; liberty for the poor; curing of illnesses; bad spirits being driven out; bringing spiritual wholeness and preaching the good news; etc. These things will never happen as perfectly as they should in this phase when Satan is still "The prince of this world." They can only be fully realised during the

# Learning to lead for the Kingdom

Reign of Christ when Satan is in prison; but as Jesus' followers, we strive to be the light of the world and the salt of the earth so that our world may reflect something of the goodness of God; something of the nature of the true Kingdom of God when Christ is in charge. We will expand more on the third and eternal phases later. For now, our focus is on the second phase.

The Kingdom of God in this second phase operates in an environment that is still dominated by "The prince of this world", Satan, the devil to whom we surrendered the kingdom when we disobeyed God. Consequently, this is a time for the Sower when the farmer sows the Word of God and it is received in different ways. There are those who hear the Word and the devil takes it away. There are those on rocky ground who hear the Word but have no roots and cannot bear fruit. There are those who receive the Word but are choked by concerns such as worries, riches or pleasures of this world. But there are also those on good soil who hear the Word, keep it and persevere in the face of all worries, temptations and pleasures. These bear fruit. (See Luke 8: 5-15). Those who bear fruit can be said to have the kingdom "Within them." The fruit they bear is a result of the values and characteristics of the Kingdom being manifested in their thoughts, words and deeds.

Despite difficulties, impediments and contradictions, the Kingdom of God continues to grow in this world. As citizens of the Kingdom and witnesses of Christ, we pray that the Kingdom continues to grow like a mustard seed which is the smallest of all seeds, but becomes a big tree on whose branches birds come to perch. We pray that the Kingdom grows and impacts the world like yeast that a woman takes and mixes into twenty seven kilograms of flour until it works through all the

# The Restoration of the Kingdom - Jesus and His Mission

dough. (See Luke 13:18-21). That is the way we want the Kingdom to impact the world. Consequently, we have a duty to promote the advancement of the Kingdom, to work for the spreading of the gospel throughout the world.

In this second phase of the kingdom, Satan and his angels are working day and night to deceive the world – to lead many away from the faith; to bring untold suffering among the poor; to cause politicians to worship power and wealth at the expense of the people; to perpetuate injustice and oppression; to promote immorality, corruption and sinfulness. The world's values are the values of Babylon, the Prostitute, as depicted in Revelations 17 and 18. As messengers of Christ, we pray and act that the world may feel the positive effects of the values of the Kingdom; that the world gets transformed by the Kingdom and becomes a better world in which people are liberated from extreme forms of oppression; in which there is more justice; there is more care for the poor and suffering; people experience spiritual healing; and more and more people hear the Word and do what they are supposed to do in obedience to God.

What we are praying for here, is not a perfect world, but a world that more accurately mirrors the world of the Kingdom of God, the kind of world that Jesus had in mind when He announced "The Kingdom of God is near." As indicated above, Satan is still active, but the forces of good are gaining more ground. Although arguing from a somewhat different perspective, Albert Nolan (1992: 61) puts it this way: "The difference is between a community of humankind in which evil reigns supreme and a community of humankind in which

25

goodness reigns supreme." We know that goodness cannot reign supreme until Jesus comes as King, but we pray and strive for the light of Christ to be seen in the world. In this regard, our phase may be called the *Transitional Phase*. It is transitional in the sense that Jesus has put in place structures, processes and value systems that enable the world to know and understand what is required to enter the Kingdom of God.

The phase can be likened to a transitional government in a country that was a colony and is being prepared for full nationhood, but has not yet been granted full independence. The citizens of that nation have a taste of what it means to be an independent state, but are still subjects of the former colonial power.

*Some Characteristics of the Second Phase of the Kingdom*

The second phase comes after the period of the patriarchs and the prophets. The period of the Patriarchs (Abraham, Isaac and Jacob), the Law of Moses and the Prophets can be referred to as the *Preparatory Phase* during which God was preparing for the coming of the Saviour into the world. During this period, God was building the nation of Israel, developing an environment in which it would be possible for "the Prophet" promised to Moses would be able to come and speak God's Words. This would be in the second or *Transitional* phase of the Kingdom. This brings us to another dimension of the second phase:

In this second or transitional phase, the kingdom has not "Fully come;" it has only "Come near" for the following and other reasons:

1. The Son of God Himself, the Redeemer, has come into the world, died for us and shown us the way to

# The Restoration of the Kingdom - Jesus and His Mission

the Father; but we who are alive do not see Him face-to-face, even though we know that He is with us "To the end of the age", meaning "To the end of this phase of the Kingdom".

2. God has been revealed by the Son, but we who are alive do not see God's face.

3. We have been saved by the blood of Jesus, but we are still subject to the temptations of Satan.

4. In this phase of the Kingdom, Christ rules in the hearts of those who believe in Him, who have been baptized with water and the Spirit and been born again; who have become citizens of the Kingdom and continue to pray and work for the spreading of the Kingdom. They have the Kingdom "Within them." However, the struggle between good and evil persists unabated; Satan continues to deceive many, with some exhibiting the characteristics of seed that falls on rocky ground or among thorns. There are many false prophets, with some claiming "I am He. The time is near" (Luke 21:8). Satan and his angels have not yet accepted the Lordship and Kingship of Christ. Furthermore, in this phase, it is not every knee that shall bow, and not every tongue that shall confess that Jesus Christ is King.

5. Christ indeed came to heal the broken hearted; to proclaim liberty to captives and freedom to those in prison; and to bring good news to the poor. However, there is still a lot of suffering in the world; there are oppressive and despotic governments; nations are waging wars against each other; and many are

persecuted for confessing Christ and for upholding the values of the Kingdom.

6.  Israel has not yet accepted Jesus Christ as the promised Messiah, and Israelites are still scattered all over the world, although almost two thousand years since the inception of this second phase, the state of Israel was set up.

In summary, what we can say about our present phase of the Kingdom is that before the first coming of Christ, we were behind a dark veil where we did not have even a glimmer of the Kingdom of God. Now that it has "come near" we can see it as if in a mirror, as it were. We cannot see it fully as we shall see it in the reign of Christ and the eternal phase of the Kingdom. The Apostle Paul puts it succinctly when he says, "For now we see only a reflection as in a mirror; then we shall see face to face" (1 Corinthians 13:12). In this phase, we see the Kingdom with the eyes of faith. As again Paul puts it, "For we live by faith, not by sight" (2 Corinthians 5:7).

## The Third Phase: The Coming of the Kingdom of God on Earth

### The Establishment of the Kingdom of God – the Millennium

The Third Phase is the Reign of Christ on earth, otherwise called the Millennium (meaning a thousand years). This is the main era that the Christians of all ages have been praying for when they pray "Thy Kingdom come", although they may not fully understand what this Kingdom is. This is what the early Christians were looking forward to, and they were clear they were waiting for the reign of Christ. The Gospels quote Jesus

# The Restoration of the Kingdom - Jesus and His Mission

referring to this, His reign, on a number of occasions. One of the occasions was during His trial when the high priest asked Him, "Are you the Messiah, the Son of the Blessed One?", Jesus responded without any equivocation: "I am", said Jesus. "And you will see the Son of Man sitting at the right hand of the Mighty One and coming on the clouds of heaven"(Mark 14:61-62). When Peter asked him what reward they who had followed Him were going to receive, His response was clear and unambiguous: "Truly I tell you, at the renewal of all things, when the Son of Man sits on His glorious throne, you who have followed Me will also sit on twelve thrones, judging the twelve tribes of Israel" (Matthew 19:28).

But how will Jesus' reign on earth come about? We get the answer from the Book of Revelation and from the Prophet Zechariah. From Revelation (19:11-21), we learn that Jesus will come riding a white horse. As He has been faithful to His Father and came into the world to testify to the truth (John 18:37), He is called "Faithful and True," and His name is "The Word of God." He has now come to wage war, but He does so with justice, just as He judges with justice. When He first came, He was defenceless as He was in a Kingdom that was not God's kingdom (See John 18:36). This time, the armies of heaven follow Him riding on white horses. On His robe and His thigh are written the words "KING OF KINGS AND LORD OF LORDS." The armies of the kings of the earth that will have come to fight Him will be killed; the beast and the false prophet will be captured. In Revelation 20 we see that the dragon, namely Satan, is thrown into the Abyss where he is imprisoned for one thousand years. This is the Battle of Armageddon referred to in Revelation 16:16, where Christ will be fighting the Anti-Christ (the beast) and the false prophet, who, together with their armies are agents of the dragon (Satan or the devil). Armageddon is present day Mount Megiddo in Israel. At the same time, the saints come to life and will reign with Christ for one thousand years.

The promise that Jesus made to His disciples that they would sit on twelve thrones seems to be fulfilled here: "I saw thrones on which were seated those who had been given authority to judge" (Revelation 20:4). It may well be that the twelve are not the only ones who will be given authority to judge, but from what Jesus said to them, it is reasonable to conclude they will be among the judges.

Zechariah 14 gives us more information about the day of Christ's victory: First, He will stand on the Mount of Olives from which He ascended to heaven after His resurrection. And when He comes, He will come with "All the holy ones" who, we now know from Revelation, will reign with Him for one thousand years. The Lord will strike all the nations that fought against Jerusalem with a plague, and on that day, the Lord will establish a theocracy over all the earth. After the establishment of the reign of Christ, "The survivors from all the nations that have attacked Jerusalem will go up year after year to worship the King, the LORD Almighty, and to celebrate the Festival of Tabernacles." Those nations that will refuse to go up and take part in the Festival will have no rain. It is also in Zechariah that we see the Israelites repenting for not accepting Jesus as Messiah who is now their Saviour against the nations that are gathered to destroy Israel (See Zechariah 12:10 -13). We will return to the repentance and conversion of the Israelites later in my discussion of Jerusalem and the bride of Christ. The important issue here, is to point out that Israel will be part of the Kingdom of God during the millennium.

## *The Characteristics of the Millennium Kingdom of God*

What kind of ruler will Jesus be? He will be the kind of ruler all people would love to have: Isaiah tells us he will be called: "Wonderful Counsellor, Mighty God, Everlasting Father, Prince of Peace. Of the greatness of His government and peace there will be no end. He will reign on David's throne and over His kingdom, establishing and upholding it with justice and righteousness…" (Isaiah 9:6-7).

What is more, He will have the Spirit of wisdom and understanding, of counsel, of knowledge and fear of the Lord (See Isaiah 11:2). The majority of the people of the world in our time, in this Phase 2 of the Kingdom, suffer from the effects of injustice, cruelty, selfishness and other ills of those who rule them. In Christ, we will have a very different kind of ruler. As Ruler, Jesus will not only be a wise Ruler and a Father, who is a Counsellor to those who have problems and brings peace to all, His emphasis on justice and righteousness will be underpinned by the highest degree of objectivity and fairness: "He will not judge by what he sees with his eyes, or decide by what he hears with his ears; but with righteousness he will judge the needy, with justice he will give decisions for the poor of the earth" (Isaiah 11: 3b-4).

And how will the reign of Christ, the Kingdom of God on earth, impact on the quality of life for the people in the Kingdom? The incredible thing is that it is not only human beings that will benefit from the reign of Christ. We noted in Genesis 1 that in God's original Kingdom on earth, all living creatures were meant to give glory to God under the leadership of humankind. The implication here, is that there was supposed to be harmony between humankind and all living things. This state of affairs is what we see in the Kingdom of God on earth. But there is more: There is harmony among all living things – human beings, wild animals, snakes etc. Thus, the Wolf will live with the Lamb; Cows and Lions will move about together and will be led by a child; the young of a Cow and that of a Bear will lie together; a human infant will play next to the living place of a Cobra… This is because the whole earth will be filled with the knowledge of God "As the waters cover the sea." The values of the Kingdom will have such great impact that all creation will be filled with the goodness of God. (See Isaiah 11:6-9). Furthermore, there will be no carnivorous animals and no poisonous snakes as "The lion will eat straw like the Ox and dust will be the serpent's food" (Isaiah 65:25).

There will be absolute peace; the land will be productive; and those who live in houses will be secure, just as they will enjoy the fruits of their labour, as no one will deprive another person of their possessions (See Isaiah 65:21-22). Furthermore, Christ the King will be a unifier as "The nations will rally to Him" (Isaiah 11:10). As for the Israelites, the Lord "Will reach out his hand a second time to reclaim the surviving remnant of His people from Assyria, from Lower Egypt, from Upper Egypt, from Cush, from Elam, from Babylonia, from Hamath and from the islands of the Mediterranean." Any jealousies between the twelve tribes of Israel will be gone. The Lord will be working for both the gentiles and the Israelites: "He will raise a banner for the nations and gather the exiles of Israel."

# The Restoration of the Kingdom - Jesus and His Mission

The reference to the Lord "Reaching out His hand a second time to reclaim the surviving remnant of His people" could have a double meaning. It certainly refers to the liberation of the Israelites from the Pharaoh of Egypt as the first time; but it could also refer to the fact that the Lord brought His people to Israel in 1948, and will now be reclaiming from foreign lands the remaining Israelites who did not go back to their homeland in 1948 when the state of Israel was re-established after about 1878 years of its non-existence.

## The End of the Third Phase

Three major events will take place when the millennium comes to a close. First, Satan will be released from the Abyss for a short while and will yet again try to rally the nations against the kingdom of God. The fighters will be devoured by a fire, and Satan will be captured and thrown into the lake of burning fire, where he, the Anti-Christ and the false prophet will be tormented for ever and ever. Second, the earth and the heavens will disappear from the presence of the Lord. Third, all the dead will be judged by Christ. Those whose names will not be found in the book of life will be thrown into the lake of fire. The others will go to the new earth. Finally, death and Hades will be thrown into the lake of fire, and that will be the end of death.

# Learning to lead for the Kingdom

## The *Final and Eternal Phase of the Kingdom*

*The New Heaven and the New Earth*

The fourth and eternal phase of the Kingdom of God comes at the end of the world: "When the Son of Man comes in His glory, and all the angels with Him, He will sit on His glorious throne" (Matthew 25:31). This is the judgement time when the Lord will separate the sheep from the goats as was prophesied by Ezekiel: "I will judge between one sheep and another, and between rams and goats" (Ezekiel 34:17). The earth and the heavens have now fled from Jesus sitting on His glorious judgement throne to judge all the dead. There is no more place for the earth and the heavens as we know them now. They are not part of the new order which comes about after the millennium and the day of final judgement. Referring to this new order, Jesus tells John, "I am making everything new!" (Revelation 21:5). Nothing is left as it was. This is what Jesus meant when He told His disciples, "Truly I tell you, at the renewal of all things, when the Son of Man sits on His glorious throne, you who have followed Me will also sit on twelve thrones, judging the twelve tribes of Israel" (Matthew 19:28).

There are two important points to remember here: First, there is nothing that is left untouched by the renewal – even heaven is transformed because this is *the renewal of all things*. Second, the end of the judgement process is followed by the rewarding of all human beings according to what they have done. Accordingly, "'Then the King will say to those on His right, 'Come, you who are blessed by my Father; take your inheritance, the Kingdom prepared for you since the creation of the world...'" (Matthew 25:34). In like manner, "'Then he

# The Restoration of the Kingdom - Jesus and His Mission

will say to those on His left, 'Depart from Me, you who are cursed, into the eternal fire prepared for the devil and his angels.'" When we open the next chapter of Revelation, we are ushered into "A new heaven and a new earth," and if we follow John's vision, we are invited to see the Holy City, the new Jerusalem, "Coming down out of heaven from God, prepared as a bride, beautifully dressed for her husband" (Revelation 21:2). Jesus has completed His work as the Christ, the Son of the living God, and the Saviour of all humankind. He has defeated all His enemies, including death. We have now come to the point of which Paul says, "Then the end will come, when He hands over the Kingdom to God the Father after He has destroyed all dominion, authority and power" (1 Corinthians 15:24).

It has been a titanic struggle for Jesus, beginning with His birth as a human baby in Bethlehem; growing up among humans; introducing the kingdom of God to humanity and training His apostles; suffering and being crucified; rising from the dead and going back to the Father; establishing the Christian Church through the Holy Spirit; coming back to earth as Conqueror and King; defeating all His enemies; judging the living and the dead; and handing the Kingdom over to the Father. In this whole journey, He has saved humankind and restored the Kingdom originally lost to humanity. He is the new Adam through whom we regain the kingdom we lost. This, then, is the final destiny of mother earth, and the destiny of humankind – the final restoration of the kingdom we lost as a result of the sin of Adam. This is where the world is going, whether we like it or not; whether we believe it or not. So, there will be a new heaven and a new earth "For the first heaven and

35

the first earth had passed away, and there was no longer any sea" (Revelation 21:1). Jerusalem, the Holy City, will shine with the glory of God. More importantly, God will be with His people at last:

'And I heard a loud voice from the throne saying, "Look, God's dwelling place is now among the people, and he will dwell with them. They will be his people, and God himself will be with them and be their God. He will wipe every tear from their eyes. There will be no more death or mourning or crying or pain, for the old order of things has passed away" (Rev 21:3-4).

This is a fulfilment of the prophecy of Isaiah: "See, I will create new heavens and a new earth. The former things will not be remembered, nor will they come to mind. But be glad and rejoice forever in what I will create, for I will create Jerusalem to be a delight and its people a joy. I will rejoice over Jerusalem and take delight in my people; the sound of weeping and of crying will be heard in it no more." (Isaiah 65:17-19).

The earth will no longer be just an extension of the Kingdom of God, but will be part of the heavenly Kingdom of God since "God's dwelling place is now among the people." There is a marriage of heaven and earth in this new order. For citizens of the Kingdom, the end of the world is ultimately a time of everlasting joy. As Peter puts it, this is a time we should look forward to: "But in keeping with His promise we are looking forward to a new heaven and a new earth, where righteousness dwells" (2 Peter 3:13). As Peter himself admits (See 2 Peter 15-16), Paul writes about these things "With the wisdom that God gave him." Of particular interest in what Paul writes are the following points: First, Paul shows the link

# The Restoration of the Kingdom - Jesus and His Mission

between Adam and Christ, which is the link between the first and final phases of the kingdom. Through Adam, we lost the Kingdom of God; through Jesus Christ the Kingdom will be ours for eternity. We will have regained what we lost through our disobedience: "For since death came through a man, the resurrection of the dead comes also through a man. For as in Adam all die, so in Christ all will be made alive. But each in turn: Christ the firstfruits; then, when he comes, those who belong to Him. Then the end will come, when He hands over the Kingdom to God the Father after He has destroyed all dominion, authority and power ...The last enemy to be destroyed is death" (1 Corinthians 15:21-26). At this stage, surely, "Every knee should bow ... and every tongue acknowledge that Jesus Christ is Lord" (Philippians 2:10).

Paul also explains how the resurrection will take place and why we cannot enter the Kingdom of God with our natural bodies, and consequently, why our earthly bodies must die and return to dust: "I declare to you, brothers and sisters, that flesh and blood cannot inherit the Kingdom of God, nor does the perishable inherit the imperishable. Listen, I tell you a mystery: We will not all sleep, but we will all be changed – in a flash, in the twinkling of an eye, at the last trumpet. For the trumpet will sound, the dead will be raised imperishable, and we will be changed. For the perishable must clothe itself with the imperishable, and the mortal with immortality" (1 Corinthians 15: 50-53). It is important to note what is happening here: There are two processes which make human bodies fit for heaven: Those who have died in Christ will be raised to new life with imperishable bodies fit for the kingdom of God.

Those who are alive will be changed in a flash, with their mortal bodies transformed to immortal.

In 1 Thessalonians 4, Paul describes what will happen to those who have died, and those who will still be alive at the second coming of Jesus: "For the Lord himself will come down from heaven, with a loud command, with the voice of the archangel and with the trumpet call of God, and the dead in Christ will rise first. After that, we who are still alive and are left will be caught up together with them in the clouds to meet the Lord in the air" (1 Thessalonians 4:16-17).

This has given rise to a big debate about the "Rapture theory", the idea of the elect being taken up to heaven in the same way that Jesus ascended to heaven after His resurrection. (See, for instance Hindson & Hitchcock (2017). Will the rapture occur before, after, or during the tribulation? In other words, is it the *pre-tribulation,* or the *post-tribulation* or the *mid-tribulation* theory that is correct? It could be argued that for believing and genuine followers of Jesus Christ, the important issue is that from then on, we will be with the Lord forever. It is a time of final liberation from the woes of the world we currently live in.

Some scholars have advanced convincing arguments in favour of the "pre-tribulation rapture" theory, the view that Jesus will first come *before* the tribulation, to take His own to heaven before the terror and misery associated with the end times He predicted in the gospels (See Luke 21:5-36; Matthew 24:1-51). In these passages, Jesus was talking about both the end times and the destruction of Jerusalem by the Romans in the year 70. In terms of the end times, the pre-tribulation rapture theory suggests that Jesus' Second Coming will be in

# The Restoration of the Kingdom - Jesus and His Mission

two stages: First, He will come unannounced to take His faithful followers who will be "caught up together with them (i.e. with the risen dead) in the clouds to meet the Lord in the air" (See 1 Thessalonians 4:14-17). Both the living and risen dead saints will now be safe with the Lord. The Lord will then come again to judge the world (See, for instance, Hindson & Hitchcock 2017:101-112). On his part Bryant Wright (2017:123) suggests that "A rapture of the church will occur sometime before Jesus' second coming." He gives the analogy of Noah's ark which was lifted up above the floods to escape God's judgement. When He had finished judging the unrighteous, so to speak, the ark was lowered down. In the same way, the church will be raised "To the wedding feast in heaven with Jesus while God brings judgement on the earth during the Great Tribulation." Then when Christ's judgement of the world is completed during His second coming, "The church is lowered back down to the earth to reign with Him" (Ibid:144). Wright's wedding feast idea is mostly based on Revelations 19:6-9. LaHaye and Hindson (2015:133-134) are of the same view with regard to the wedding. The visions that Jesus showed the End-Times prophetess, Choo Nam Thomas (2006: 60-61; 139-141; 249-250) support the pre-tribulation theory. On page 60, Choo Nam asks, "Lord, when will the tribulation occur?" Jesus' response is, "*After I bring My children to My Kingdom*".

What also becomes clear is that the tribulation and the end of the world are not the same event. In common discourse, we tend to talk as if the tribulation will be immediately followed by the end of the world. According to the Book of Revelation, there is at least a thousand years before the earth and the heavens flee from Jesus Christ seated on His seat of judgement seat (See Revelation 20: 7-15). I have also asked myself whether the members of the church who reign with Christ during the millennium will also have to appear before the judgment seat of Christ at the end of the world. The answer is given in Paul's letter to the Corinthians: "For we must all appear before the judgement seat of Christ, so that each of us may receive what is due us for the things done while in the body, whether good or bad" (2 Corinthians 5:10). What this means is, there is no exception on that day. All of us, whether saved or not, must appear before Jesus when He judges all human beings on the last day. This view is supported by Choo Nam Thomas' evidence (Ibid 249): "The Lord told me so often that whoever is raptured will have to stand before the judgment seat before the wedding takes place."

### *The Restoration of Eden*

Going back to Genesis, we notice how Adam and Eve were prevented from eating the tree of life (See Genesis 3:22). In this way, humans became mortal. Their bodies became perishable. In the final phase of the Kingdom, the citizens will be raised from the dead and their bodies transformed from perishable to imperishable. Just as the Lord was raised and went to heaven in a new glorious body, we shall also be raised with glorified bodies. There will be no more death since, through Jesus Christ, death will be finally defeated as prophesied by Isaiah (Isaiah 25:8) and Hosea (Hosea 13:14). Hence Paul echoes these prophesies: "Death has been swallowed up in victory." "Where, O death, is your victory? Where, O death, is your sting?" (1 Corinthians 15: 54-55).

# The Restoration of the Kingdom - Jesus and His Mission

Adam and Eve were banished from the Garden of Eden (See Genesis 3:23-24), and in that regard humans became "Restless wanderers on the earth" like Cain (Genesis 4:12-14), but in the final phase Eden will be restored, and the tree of life will be there "For the healing of the nations." The river which in the first phase watered the garden from Eden (See Genesis 2:10), will in the final phase become the river of the water of life flowing from the throne of God and of the Lamb "Down the middle of the great street of the city" (Revelation 22:1-2). We will first experience the Kingdom of God during the one thousand year reign of Christ, and we will obviously see Him as we will reign with Him, but it is not clear whether we will see God fully during the millennium. It is in the new earth that we can experience the full manifestation of the Kingdom of God on this planet; when we can see God's face; when in the fullest sense of the word we are God's people and He is our God. We will then not just live by faith, but by sight as well (See 2 Corinthians 5:7) because we will be fully in the Kingdom: body, soul and spirit. Whereas, "For now we see only a reflection as in a mirror; then we shall see face to face" (1 Corinthians 13:12). This is the final and eternal phase of the Kingdom of God where we shall have the eternal life that Jesus promised to all who believe in Him, after the final defeat of Satan and his angels who will be thrown into the lake of burning sulphur forever and ever (See Revelation 20:10); and death has been defeated and also thrown into the lake of fire (See Revelation 20:14).

At this stage and during the reign of Christ, humans will be back here on our transformed Mother Earth, which God created for us and which we had lost to the devil. While the

41

elect who have died before the millennium will be received in the Kingdom of God in heaven, the final destiny of humankind at the end of this world and in the reign of Christ will be here on earth. It is appropriate to quote the Psalmist again: "The highest heavens belong to the LORD, but the earth He has given to mankind" (Psalm 115:16). When we have been raised from the dead, the Garden of Eden from which we were banished when Adam and Eve sinned against God (See Genesis 3:23-24) will be ours again (See Revelation 22:1-5). Jerusalem will be the beautiful, strong and prosperous city that the prophets and the psalmists spoke about (See Psalm 122; Psalm 137:5-6). The nations will walk by its light, and it will enjoy the glory and honour of the nations (See Revelation 21:22-27). It is reasonable to suggest that there will be a new and closer relationship between heaven and earth at this stage of the kingdom, since "The throne of God and of the Lamb will be in the city..." i.e. in Jerusalem (See Revelation 22:3). There is therefore, a marriage of heaven and earth. John Eldredge (2017:175) puts it even more forcefully: "Better said, we get heaven *and* earth; both realms of God's Kingdom come together at the renewal of all things."

### *Reflections on the New Jerusalem and the Bride of Christ*

*The Place of Jerusalem in the Eternal Phase of the Kingdom*

There is something of a controversy about what the New Jerusalem stands for here. Some theologians identify the New Jerusalem with the Church of Christ. The great authority on the Book of Revelation, William Hendriksen (1940, 1967:218) contends, "This new and holy Jerusalem is very clearly the

# The Restoration of the Kingdom - Jesus and His Mission

Church of the Lord Jesus Christ, as is also evident from the fact that it is here and elsewhere called the bride…" This is a matter we shall return to in the next chapter when we comment on the relationship between the Christian church and the kingdom of God. Here our focus is on Jerusalem with regard to its place in "The New Heaven and "The New Earth". What Hendriksen says about the Church of Christ becoming the New Jerusalem may well be true, but taken literally in the way Hendriksen puts it, the interpretation presents a problem about the place of Jerusalem in "The New Heaven" and "The New Earth." Jerusalem is indeed the "Bride and wife of the Lamb" (Revelation 21:9). The question that arises is what has then happened to the Jerusalem which is referred to so often both in the Old and the New Testament, if the Church becomes the New Jerusalem? Does it fizzle out into nothing? Is Jerusalem not "the City of David" that has been recreated and renewed like everything else and become the Holy City? Is Jerusalem not the city that the Lord said it shall be inhabited (See Isaiah 44:24-28), and Zion the city in which His afflicted people shall find refuge (See Isaiah 14:32)? Zion and Jerusalem's glory is predicted In Isaiah 54, 60, 62 and 65, and echoes of the Book of Revelation are found in some of these, as we shall see below.

When Jesus wept over Jerusalem and said to her "I tell you, you will not see me again until you say 'Blessed is he who comes in the name of the Lord'" (Luke 13:34-35) was He only referring to His triumphant entry on a donkey (See Matthew 21:1-11), or was He also referring to His final return as the Alpha and the Omega, the First and the Last, the Beginning and the End, and as the Root and Offspring of David and the

# Learning to lead for the Kingdom

Bright Morning Star (See Revelation 22:12-16). This Jerusalem that killed the prophets and the Saviour Himself; this Jerusalem that was destroyed by the Romans in Year 70, and whose house is "Left to you desolate" (Luke 12:35); is this not the recreated Jerusalem in the New Earth that comes down out of heaven as "The Holy City", and "The bride, the wife of the Lamb?" (Revelation 21:2). We need to look more closely at the Bible to answer this question and to examine further Hendriksen's position.

The prophet Zechariah prophesied about a day when all the nations will be gathered to fight against Jerusalem (See Zechariah 14). The city will be captured, its houses ransacked and its women raped. However, the Lord will fight on behalf of Jerusalem. Finally, Jerusalem will be raised up high and will remain in place: "It will be inhabited; never again will it be destroyed. Jerusalem will be secure" (Zechariah 14:11). Bryant Wright (2017) has argued that this is a prophecy about the place referred to as Armageddon in Revelations 16:16, which is present day Mount Meggido in Israel. The kings of the world will be gathered together at this place "On the great day of God Almighty" for battle against Israel. They will be acting on behalf of the dragon (Satan), the beast (the Anti-Christ) and the false prophet (See Revelation 16:13-14). In chapters 16-18 of his book, Wright has presented a fascinating and convincing account of how the gathering there will be to destroy Israel once and for all, ostensibly in the name of "World peace". The armies of the united forces of these nations will be led by the Anti-Christ. By this time, Israel will have no allies – even America will have deserted the Jewish nation.

44

# The Restoration of the Kingdom - Jesus and His Mission

Facing the disaster prophesied in Zechariah 14, the people of Israel will have no other solution but to turn to God and pray to Him to send the Messiah they have always believed in. The Messiah will indeed come to save Israel, but this Messiah will turn out to be Jesus. It is at this point that the people of Israel as a nation will repent and accept Jesus as their Messiah; and Jesus will save them both physically (By saving Jerusalem and its people) and spiritually (For they will now repent and earn the salvation that is earned by all who believe in Jesus). This time, He is not riding a lowly foal of a donkey as He did when He first entered Jerusalem as King (See Luke 19:28-44), but is on a white horse and on His robe and thigh are written the words "KING OF KINGS AND LORD OF LORDS" (Revelation 19:11-16). It is surely at this point that Jerusalem will, for the second time, cry out "Blessed is He who comes in the name of the Lord" (Luke 13:35). The victory of Jesus over His enemies has already been discussed. Now, where does this place Jerusalem and the Christian Church in "The New Heaven" and "The New Earth"?

Through prayer and reflection, I have come to the conclusion that following the renewal of the earth at the end of the world, the new Jerusalem will neither be just the church nor just the city of Jerusalem. The new Jerusalem will be a combination of Jerusalem and the Church of Christ, the Church being those Christians who have been found worthy of the Kingdom of God. The evidence for this is in Revelation 21:12-14: "It (i.e. Jerusalem) had a great high wall with twelve gates, and with twelve angels at the gates. On the gates were written the names of the twelve tribes of Israel. There were three gates on the east, three on the north, three on the south and three on the west. The wall of the city had twelve foundations, and on them were the names of the twelve apostles of the Lamb."

Earlier on we discussed the "Rapture" of the Church at the time of the Great Tribulation. That Jerusalem will survive was prophesied by Zechariah (Zechariah 14:11). So, both the Church and Jerusalem will survive the tribulation. The twelve gates shown to the Apostle John in Revelation 21:12-13 are the same gates prophesied by Ezekiel (Ezekiel 48:30-35) except that in Ezekiel the names of the twelve tribes are given together with the positions of their gates: on the north: the gates of Reuben, Judah and Levi; on the east: the gates of Joseph, Benjamin and Dan; on the south the gates of Simeon, Issachar and Zebulun; and on the west: the gates of Gad, Asher and Naphtali. The foundations of the walls of the new Jerusalem have the names of the twelve Apostles. The picture that emerges here, is clear: While the foundations of the new Jerusalem are based on the Church of Jesus Christ as represented by the twelve founders of the Church; the gates are based on the twelve tribes of Israel. This resolves the puzzle of the Church and the new Jerusalem. The new Jerusalem has the Church of Jesus Christ as its foundation; but its gates come from the people of Israel, the chosen people. The new Jerusalem is therefore, based on the truth of God as revealed in both the Old Testament and the New Testament. The new Jerusalem signifies the fulfilment of the Law and the Prophets by Jesus.

There is yet another significance to the new Jerusalem: We saw earlier that in the first phase there was a river which flowed from Eden and watered the garden. In the new earth, "The

# The Restoration of the Kingdom - Jesus and His Mission

river of the water of life" flows from the throne of God and the Lamb "Down the middle of the great street of the city" (Revelation 22:1-2). In this regard, the new Jerusalem can be seen as the new Paradise. In other words, the new Jerusalem is Eden restored and renewed in the kingdom of God. This is the sense in which we can clearly see the movement and development of human history. The history and actions of humanity started in Eden, and all events in history are leading to the Kingdom of God, which, on earth, will have its centre or, shall we say, its "Headquarters" in the new Jerusalem. It is also reasonable to suggest that in the final phase of the Kingdom of God, there is one kingdom encompassing both heaven and the earth. For human beings the centre of the Kingdom will be in Jerusalem, as "The throne of God and of the Lamb will be in the city" (Revelation 22:3).

## The Wedding and the Bride of Christ

In all the literature that I have read, the wedding is assumed to take place in Chapter 19 of Revelation. This is before Jesus has defeated the Anti-Christ (the beast) and the false prophet; before the imprisonment of Satan in the Abyss; and consequently before the reign of Christ on earth or the millennium. The logic of this argument is that the Church is raptured before the tribulation and Jesus gets married to His bride, the Church, in heaven before He comes back to defeat His enemies and to establish the Kingdom of God on earth. There is a need to take a closer look at the Scriptures and the facts here.

# Learning to lead for the Kingdom

First, we note that the wedding in Revelation 19 is introduced suddenly as if it is something that has been referred to before which the reader should already be aware of. This is in fact the case. The wedding is glorified in Isaiah 62, which highlights the splendour of Jerusalem. Because the basic translation I have used for this book, the New International Version, uses un-translated names for key words in the text, I will use the New Jerusalem Bible which makes the meaning immediately clear: "The nations will then see your saving justice, and all kings your glory, and you will be called a new name which Yahweh's mouth will reveal. You will be a crown of splendour in Yahweh's hand, a princely diadem in the hand of your God.

No more will you be known as 'Forsaken' or your country be known as 'Desolation'; instead, you will be called 'My Delight is in her' and your country 'The Wedded'; for Yahweh will take delight in you and your country will have its wedding. Like a young man marrying a virgin, your rebuilder will wed you, and as the bridegroom rejoices in his bride, so will your God rejoice in you" (Isaiah 62:2-5 NJB)

In suggesting that Revelation 19:7-8 is about the wedding of Christ and the Christian Church, commentators are guided mainly by Ephesians 5:23-33 where the church is presented as the bride of Christ. This key passage may be understood to be strengthened by Colossians 1:22 which I quote: "But now He has reconciled you by Christ's physical body through death to present you holy in His sight, without blemish and free from accusation…" There is no disputing the idea of the marriage between Christ and the Church in the text above. The problem is that this marriage is assumed by Christian theologians to take

# The Restoration of the Kingdom - Jesus and His Mission

place in Revelation 19 where the church is then equated to the bride of the Lamb mentioned there. But what seems to be happening is this: In the Old Testament we hear the Lord rejoicing in Jerusalem's *future marriage* when her builder will wed her. This is a desolate and forsaken Jerusalem that is turned into the bridegroom's bride and the Lord's delight in the Book of Revelation. If we put Ephesians 5 and Isaiah 62 together, we get the following picture: In the *Transitional Phase* of the kingdom, the age of the Christian Church, Christ is married to his church. In the *Final Phase*, the Lamb brings about the marriage promised to the people of Israel in the prophecy of Isaiah when they were promised "The country will have its wedding" and shall be called "The Wedded". We also note that in Revelation 19 the name of the bride is not given; we are not told who the bride is; but Revelation 21 is clear and unequivocal: "I saw the Holy City, the new Jerusalem, coming down out of heaven from God, prepared as a bride beautifully dressed for her husband" (Revelation 21:2). And when one of the seven angels who had the bowls full of the seven last plagues says to John, "Come, I will show you the bride, the wife of the Lamb", what does John see? He is carried away in the Spirit by the angel to a great mountain where he is shown "The Holy City, Jerusalem, coming down out of heaven from God" (Revelation 21:9). This shows clearly that the bride of the Lamb is the new Jerusalem.

As already explained, the new Jerusalem is a combination of Israel (Represented by the twelve tribes of Israel) and the Christian Church (Represented by the twelve apostles of Jesus). This to me explains the identity of the twenty-four elders that keep on being referred to in the Book of Revelation.

These should be the heads of the twelve tribes of Israel and the twelve Apostles of Jesus. In view of this, it becomes clear the wedding cannot take place before the tribulation as some scholars suggest. It takes place in "The New Heaven" and "The New Earth" when Christ has conquered all His enemies and brought the Kingdom to His father. Not only does He bring the Kingdom; He also brings the bride to the Father. This is what makes theological sense. For Christ at the end of time to get married to the Christian church excluding the nation of Israel and the Jewish people would be to continue the present division between Israel and the Christian Church, which means He would not have finished the work He set out to do. This would be contrary to what Scripture says. In the Letter to the Ephesians Paul writes, "His purpose was to create in Himself one new humanity out of the two, thus making peace, and in one body to reconcile both of them to God through the cross, by which He put to death their hostility" (Ephesians 2:15b-16). And again Paul writes, "This mystery is that through the gospel the Gentiles are heirs together with Israel, members together of one body, and sharers together in the promise in Christ Jesus" (Ephesians 3:6). What this means is that in the final and eternal phase of the Kingdom, all contradictions that have existed hitherto are resolved once and for all.

### Consistency and Continuity in the Bible and the Story of Jesus

In the epilogue of Revelation, Jesus declares He is coming soon, and "Will give to each person according to what they have done." He declares He is "The Alpha and the Omega, the

# The Restoration of the Kingdom - Jesus and His Mission

First and the Last, the Beginning and the End" (Revelations 22:12-13).

The question to ask is: Does the Bible present one story? Do the beginning, the middle and the end cohere? In that regard, can Jesus rightly claim to be who He is? Is he the Messiah, and does His story relate to the beginning (Genesis), and to the Law of Moses and the Prophets? Or does He present a vision of the Kingdom of God which bears no direct relation to the principal themes of the Old Testament?

First, one thing is clear: Jesus declares from the outset the connection between His teaching, the Law of Moses and the Prophets. He did not wait to be asked about the connection. In the Sermon on the Mount he says: "Do not think I have come to abolish the Law or the Prophets; I have not come to abolish them but to fulfil them... Therefore, anyone who sets aside one of the least of these commands and teaches others accordingly will be called least in the Kingdom of heaven, but whoever practices and teaches these commands will be called great in the Kingdom of heaven..." (Matthew 5:17-20).

His quarrel with the Pharisees and the Teachers of the Law was not that they taught and observed the Law, but that they distorted the commands and turned them into human commands, thus preventing the Law from reflecting and presenting the values of the Kingdom of God. The Seven Woes (See Matthew 23: 13-36; Luke 11:49-51) can sound to some readers to be disturbingly strongly worded, but they express how strongly Jesus felt these authorities had deviated from the values of the Kingdom of God. For example, they are hypocrites who "Shut the door of the Kingdom of heaven in people's faces" (Matthew 5:13); they go to great lengths to make converts, but "When you have succeeded, you make them twice as much a child of hell as you are" (Matthew 5:15); "You give a tenth of your spices – mint, dill and cumin. But you have neglected the more important matters of the law – justice, mercy and faithfulness. You should have practiced the latter, without neglecting the former" (Matthew 5:23). Jesus therefore, sees the Pharisees and Teachers of the Law presenting a very different picture of the Kingdom of heaven from His vision of it.

With regard to the Prophets, numerous scripture passages are quoted that confirm His place in the history of the Kingdom and Salvation, as was indicated in the previous chapter, including the one He cited when He announced His mission (See Luke 4:17 -21). Some prophets may have understood the Messiah to be a political leader who would restore the Jewish monarchy; some serious scholars and academic authorities on the New Testament are of the view that Jesus might have entertained the idea that He was this kind of Messiah (e.g. Nolan 1976:129-130; 131 ff), but in this writer's view, while He might have been tempted to think that way, there is no evidence whatsoever that Jesus seriously and for any length of time, believed Himself to be that kind of Messiah. He rejected that notion when He was tempted by the devil in the wilderness (See Matthew 4: 8-10). Instead, He predicted His suffering and death on a number of occasions (See Matthew 16: 21 ff; Luke 18:31-33). The gospels do not specifically refer to Jesus seeing Himself as a king in the transitional phase of the Kingdom (i.e. in our age); but there are many passages including the Parable of the Ten Minas (See Luke 19:11-27) which show He was aware of His second

# The Restoration of the Kingdom - Jesus and His Mission

coming when He would be King over the whole earth. He did, however, confirm He was the Messiah when Peter said He was "The Messiah, the Son of the living God" (Matthew 16:13-20). But what kind of Messiah did He think He was?

An indication of the kind of Messiah Jesus thought He was in the second phase can be seen from what He and John the Baptist say. When John heard about what Matthew calls "The deeds of the Messiah" he sent his disciples to ask, "Are you the one who is to come, or should we expect someone else?" Jesus' answer was, "Go back and report to John what you hear and see: The blind receive sight, the lame walk, those who have leprosy are cleansed, the deaf hear, the dead are raised, and the good news is proclaimed to the poor. Blessed is anyone who does not stumble on account of me" (Matthew 11:2-6). Among the things John said when he saw Jesus was this: "Look, the Lamb of God, who takes away the sin of the world!" (John 1:29). There is no hint in either statement about Jesus taking over political power from the Jews or the Romans. John's statement here, is a reminder of the suffering servant of God prophesied by Isaiah who "Was led like a lamb to the slaughter"; who "Bore the sin of many, and made intercession for the transgressors" (See Isaiah 52:13-15; 53:1-12). Jesus' own message is about liberating the poor and suffering, and preaching the good news. The Jews rejected Him as the Messiah because they were expecting a strong and powerful political and religious messiah who would free them from Roman imperialism and from domination by any other nations. But Jesus' idea of liberation at His first coming went far beyond freedom from political domination and oppression.

# Learning to lead for the Kingdom

Furthermore, His mission was not confined to the Chosen People, but was intended for all nations.

The place of Jesus in the history of the Kingdom and Salvation is clearly demonstrated in the Transfiguration (See Matthew 17: 1-13) where the Law is represented by Moses and the Prophets by Elijah (See also Luke 9:28-36 and Mark 9:2-8). Some scholars are inclined to think that Jesus was thinking of setting up an earthly kingdom when He said to His disciples, "Truly I tell you, some who are standing here, will not taste death before they see the Son of Man coming in His Kingdom"(Matthew 16:28). This was after Peter had declared Him as the Messiah. In this writer's view, Jesus was referring to the Transfiguration. First, He confirmed Peter's identification of Him as the Saviour, but went on to order the disciples not to tell anyone that He was the Messiah. And "From that time on" He began to explain to His disciples that He must suffer and be killed by the chief priests and teachers of the law. It would not make sense for Him to suggest He was going to set up an earthly kingdom if He was going to be killed (Although in the same breath He said He would rise to life). Peter most probably understood Him to be intending to set up a Kingdom on earth, which is why He protested at the idea of Jesus being killed.

It was immediately after He rebuked Peter as "Satan" that He made the statement just quoted about some of them seeing the Son of Man coming in His kingdom. Then, and this is the crux of the matter, the evangelist makes the point of explaining that it was six days after Jesus had said this that He took Peter, James and John to the high mountain where He was transfigured: "There He was transfigured before them. His face shone like the sun, and His clothes became as white as the light." Then Moses and Elijah appeared talking with Jesus, and while Peter was so mesmerized that He bubbled about building three shelters, a voice came from the cloud saying, "This is my Son, in whom I am well pleased. Listen to Him!" It is not too farfetched to think that on this occasion the three disciples saw something of the future glory of Jesus in His kingdom. Consequently, it is logical to conclude that it was these three that Jesus was referring to as some who would see the Son of Man coming in His kingdom before they tasted death. In terms of this He was speaking as God's anointed Messiah, and was by no means intending to set up an earthly Kingdom in the life time of His disciples.

At this juncture we return to our study of the linkage between the Old Testament and the New Testament. First, there is that link between the Prophet whom Moses told the Israelites that, "You must listen to him" (Deuteronomy 18:15), and here is God telling the three disciples of Jesus "Listen to him!" And the transfiguration of Jesus reminds us of the thunder and lightning when God appeared on Mount Sinai (See Exodus 19). For the first time Jesus appears to His disciples, not just as their human Lord and teacher, but as the divine Son of God. And God confirms the divinity of Jesus by telling the disciples, "This is My Son, whom I love; with Him I am well pleased. Listen to Him!" The disciples were now as terrified as the Israelites were on Mount Sinai when they heard God's voice, and "They fell facedown to the ground, terrified." On Mount Sinai the Lord spoke and gave the Ten Commandments and the people acknowledged the one true God (See Exodus 19 &20). On Mount Carmel Elijah proved he was the true prophet of God and the people fell prostrate and cried "The LORD –He is God! The LORD – He is God!"(1 Kings 18-31). And now on the Mount of Transfiguration, the three disciples saw for themselves what Jesus had said six days earlier, "Truly, I tell you some who are standing here will not taste death before they see the Son of Man coming in His kingdom" (Matthew 16:28). As already indicated, Moses stands for the Law; Elijah represents the true prophet of God, just as John the Baptist was; and Jesus is not only the Son of God, but the Word of God who fulfilled the Law and the Prophets as He states in Matthew 5:17-20.

A very interesting connection is the clear echoes and references between the Book of Genesis and Revelation, as has already been discussed. Thus the creation of this present earth and of humanity is clearly and convincingly echoed in the coming into being of "The new heaven and the new earth" (See Revelation 21). In the passages already cited (1 Corinthians 15 and 1 Thessalonians 4), Paul explains the link between Adam and Jesus Christ. As already explained, Jesus clarifies the link between the Law, the Prophets and His own message of the Kingdom of God. Thus while there may be what appear to be inconsistencies and stories that may not fit well into the main theme of the Bible, and while there may be different interpretations of some passages, there is nevertheless a clear thread that runs through the Bible from Genesis to Revelation.

An issue theologians and other scripture scholars do not seem to pay sufficient attention to, is the connection between the temptation in the Garden of Eden and Jesus' temptations in the wilderness. First, this may be entirely fortuitous, but I have noted that both sets of temptations involve eating. Adam and Eve were tempted to eat of the forbidden tree and Jesus was tempted to turn stones into bread. The more important point is that both temptations involve disobeying God, or rebelling against God the Father. Before he came to the Garden of Eden, Satan had rebelled against God in heaven and had been defeated (See Isaiah 14:12-14) by loyal angels led by Michael (See Isaiah 14:12-14; Revelation 12:7-9). So, it was a cosmic war. The temptation of Adam and Eve was an extension of the war by the devil to planet earth which had been intended to give glory to God under the leadership of humankind.

Satan was victorious in Eden. He succeeded in recruiting Adam and Eve to his side against God! This is why after the *Fall* sin spread rapidly in the world beginning with the sin of murder in the first degree – when Cain murdered Abel. The world became so sinful that "The LORD regretted that He had made human beings on the earth, and His heart was deeply troubled." So troubled was the Lord He said, "I will wipe from the face of the earth the human race I have made…" (Genesis 6:6-7). Hence the flood and all that ensued (See Genesis 6-9).

But God had Plan B: "For God so loved the world that he gave his one and only Son, that whoever believes in him shall not perish but have eternal life" (John 3:16). Nevertheless, the devil was to continue with his war against God. So at the crucial moment when Jesus was about to begin His ministry, Satan made his second attempt at winning the representative of God to his side. According to Matthew's account (See Matthew 4:3-11), the devil started with food, and then went to the issue of becoming a showy messiah by doing the spectacular feat of flying down from the highest point of the temple. Impatient with Jesus' rebuttals, the devil decided to be direct – to invite Jesus to obey *him* and disobey God: "All this I will give you" he said, "if you will bow down and worship me." I shudder to think what would have happened if Jesus had been lured to obey Satan: It would have been *Paradise Lost 2!* Where would we be in relation to Salvation and the Kingdom? But, as Paul puts it, Jesus "Humbled Himself by becoming obedient to death – even death on a cross!" (See Philippians 2: 5-11).

### *The Purpose of the Analysis*

The purpose of this and the previous chapter is to provide the context in which the citizens of the Kingdom in the second phase can examine Jesus' central message with a view to understanding it more clearly in order to live it and propagate it more effectively. In this regard there is a challenge to Christian leaders and all who aspire to be leaders in propagating the Gospel message of Jesus. Does our world reflect what Jesus hoped to see in this realm or what we have called the transitional phase of the Kingdom of God? Can we identify the Kingdom of God with the Christian Church as it is today? What can the Kingdom citizens do to ensure the message of Jesus is more effectively propagated and put into practice? For us to answer these questions with any degree of adequacy, we need to have a clearer conception of Jesus' vision of the Kingdom of God, as well as a deeper understanding of the kind of Leader He was and what He taught about leadership.

# CHAPTER THREE

## Jesus' Vision of The Kingdom of God on Earth

### *Jesus as a Leader with a Vision*

A leader who wants to convince followers about the organisation, institution or whatever he/she wants to set up or achieve, must have clarity of mind about what he/she wants to do. The first requirement of a leader is therefore, to have a vision of the desired future. A leader must tell a story that convinces followers there is something worth following and working for. Jesus was a leader and must have had ideas about the project He came to set up. As we have seen, His mission was to bring back the Kingdom of God to planet earth. What was this thing going to be like? What vision did He have of this Kingdom of God that He spoke so passionately about, and for which He was prepared to lay down His life? Was it a political entity? Was it a religious organisation? Was it a human society?

It is important to remember the point already made that the Kingdom of God on earth can only be understood to be an extension of the Kingdom of God in heaven. However, the territory is different. We are here dealing with a territory where the original values of the Kingdom were lost; and with a people who had been alienated from the Kingdom of heaven. How then does Jesus see the values of the Kingdom in this territory? And how does He see the kingdom of God on earth relating to the Kingdom of God in heaven?

### *Lessons from the Sermon on the Mount*

To be able to answer the questions just asked, we need to hear from Jesus Himself. We need to analyse what He actually said about the Kingdom of God or the Kingdom of heaven. In this regard, a good starting point is the Sermon on the Mount which I once said "Sounds like a manifesto" (Ngara 2004, 53) for here we begin to have a pretty good idea about what Jesus was expecting, what was new in His teaching compared to the Law, and what impact He had on His audience. In these three chapters (Matthew 5-7), Jesus lays down what may appropriately be referred to as "norms" or "minimum standards" expected to be reflected in the character and behaviour of His followers on earth, who are the citizens of this Kingdom of God.

There is a sense in which the Kingdom of God as portrayed in the Sermon can be seen as a society or an ideal state in which people live according to the standards set by Jesus. The standards are not of human origin. They come from heaven, from God, just as the norms of the first earthly Kingdom of God in Eden were determined by God in heaven. The standards relate to issues of faith, morality, values, attitudes of mind, relations between the individual and others, as well as the role of the citizens in the broader society in which they live. From a geographical point of view this is a state

# Jesus' Vision of The Kingdom of God on Earth

without the boundaries of human countries like Nigeria, Kenya, Indonesia or Brazil. It is a supernatural state without natural boundaries. You enter the Kingdom from any point on earth when you abide by its norms, but the requirements for retaining your citizenship are very tough and strict.

In competition with the Kingdom of God on earth is another supernatural state whose norms and standards are the opposite of its own – the kingdom of Satan. The norms and values upheld in this competing Kingdom are very attractive and easy to maintain for any member of any natural state. Consequently, numerous people in our time find it much easier to abide by the principles of this other Kingdom than to follow the tough and strict norms of the Kingdom of heaven. Satan has been in charge of this Kingdom since the Fall of Humankind and is very powerful. That is why he even dared to try and recruit Jesus to his own Kingdom when he tempted Him in the desert: The evangelist shows the last temptation was the most daring of all: 'Again the devil took Him to a very high mountain and showed Him all the Kingdoms of the world and their splendour. "All this I will give you," he said, "if you will bow down and worship me."' (Matthew 4:8-9). If he can do this to the Son of God, how much more easily is he able to lure natural children of Adam and Eve? There is therefore, a perpetual struggle between the Kingdom of God and the Kingdom of Satan, and when Jesus first came to establish the Kingdom of God, the struggle must have looked like the fight between David and Goliath (See 1 Samuel 17).

As we try to understand Jesus' conception of the Kingdom of God portrayed in the Sermon on the Mount and the rest of the four Gospels, it is useful to keep this analysis in mind. It is also pertinent to remind ourselves that every state has a constitution of some kind which outlines the rights, privileges and obligations of its citizens. For the kingdom of God, the Bible is the constitution, as Myles Munroe (2006) argues. The Sermon on the Mount introduces us to various features of the constitution as presented by Jesus Who then continues to elaborate on the contents of the constitution through actions, teachings, parables, discussions and conversations. The approach used here is to start with the Sermon and then go on to expand the explanation with evidence from the rest of the gospels. We begin with Jesus' focus on the inner person.

### The Centrality of the Inner Person

One feature that becomes clear is that there is strong emphasis on the inner person. There is a new emphasis, not on outward appearances, not only on what the individual does, how he/she behaves in the sight of others, but on thoughts, values and motives that may be the origins of such deeds as adultery, murder, and hypocrisy and showing off in prayer, fasting and alms giving. Thus adultery is not just the actual act of having a sexual relationship with another person's wife or having an extra marital relationship, but also the mere fact of looking lustfully at a woman (See Matthew 5:27-30). In this regard, it can be argued that King David had already committed adultery with Batsheba before he had a physical relationship with her in bed, because he had looked lustfully at her when he saw her naked from a distance and did not resist the temptation (See 2 Samuel 11).

## Jesus' Vision of The Kingdom of God on Earth

In matters of murder, one is not only judged for the physical act of killing someone, but also gets judged for being angry with someone to the extent of calling them "Raca" or "You fool". Hence the need to be reconciled with your brother before you offer your gift at the altar (See 5:21-24).

In matters of fasting, or alms giving making a show of what you are doing with the intention of being praised by people does not please God, but makes you a hypocrite. They are also hypocrites who make a public show of their prayer and eloquently utter many words with the motive of being praised by other people. In all these cases, the reward is the praise that is given by those who see the hypocrite, as God does not reward such acts (See Matthew 6: 1-18). In matters of prayer, for example, Jesus says, "But when you pray, go into your room, close the door and pray to your Father, who is unseen. Then your Father, who sees what is done in secret, will reward you" (Matthew 6:6). At this juncture, it is pertinent to remember that one of the stern criticisms Jesus levelled against the Pharisees and Teachers of the Law was their hypocrisy and tendency to draw attention to themselves (See Matthew 23:13-36; Luke 11:49-51).

What is equally, if not more telling, about the Pharisees and Teachers of the Law, was their emphasis on external cleanliness only. Thus eating with unwashed hands was eating with "defiled hands." Hence they asked Jesus, "Why don't your disciples live according to the tradition of the elders instead of eating their food with defiled hands?" (Mark 7:5). This question gave Jesus the opportunity to explain two critical issues. First, He explained the Pharisees and Teachers of the Law had departed from the commands of God and were teaching human traditions: "You have let go of the commands and are holding on to human traditions" (Mark 7:8). Thus one of the ways in which Jesus came to fulfil the Law (See Matthew 5:17-20) was to uphold the spirit, not just the letter, of the Law. The Pharisees were concerned about the letter of the Law and consequently distorted the true meaning and intent of the commands in the Law.

The next point, which was His main response to the Jewish leaders, was to clarify the dichotomy between interiority and exteriority in matters of faith and morality; to point out where sin really originates from. Does one sin by, say, eating with unwashed hands, or even eating the meat of an animal (such as a pig) that may be considered unclean, or is it thoughts, motives, passions and desires that become the origin of sin? Thus Jesus said aloud to the crowd, "Nothing outside a person can defile them by going into them. Rather, it is what comes out of a person that defiles them" (Mark 7:15).

When later the disciples asked Him to explain His answer to the Pharisees and Teachers of the Law, He was more elaborate. First, nothing that a person eats goes to the heart. It goes to the stomach and then out of the body. He then explained: "What comes out of a person is what defiles them. For it is from within, out of a person's heart, that evil thoughts come - sexual immorality, theft, murder, adultery, greed, malice, deceit, lewdness, envy, slander, arrogance and folly. All these evils come from inside and defile a person" (Mark 7:20-23). The word "defile" has been re-defined. This is important in understanding the nature of the Kingdom of God in the second phase. It is not visual or external appearances that matter, but what is deep inside of us – in our hearts. Jesus becomes our King when He rules our hearts. This should remind us about the Lord's choice of David as future King of Israel over other sons of Jesse. In rejecting Eliab, the Lord said to Samuel, "People look at the outward appearance, but the LORD looks at the heart" (1 Samuel 16:7).

In view of the above, it is pertinent to note that Jesus associates suitability for the Kingdom of God with the inner person. To enter the Kingdom one must repent. Matthew records Jesus' first public message as "Repent, for the kingdom of heaven has come near" (Matthew 4:17). It is pertinent to repeat the explanation already made about repentance: Repentance is an internal transformation. It is a fundamental change of mind, heart and attitude that creates a new person: "Therefore, if anyone is in Christ, the new creation has come: The old has gone, the new is here!" (2 Corinthians 5:17). It is the person who has been transformed like this and become a new creation that is fit to enter the Kingdom of heaven. Undergoing this kind of transformation which makes one a new person is being born spiritually – hence, one is born again. The first birth is when one is born from the mother's womb; the second birth is when one is born of water and the Spirit. The mother gives birth to the physical person, but water and the Spirit give birth to the spiritual dimension of a human being. Hence, "Flesh gives birth to flesh, but the Spirit gives birth to spirit", Jesus told Nicodemus. Consequently, "No one can see the kingdom of God unless they are born again" (See John 3:1-8).

Repentance puts the believer in a right spiritual relationship to the Lord, so that one is not guilty before God. This is why it is not enough to seek the Kingdom of God, for seeking the Kingdom should go hand in hand with righteousness – hence, "But seek first His Kingdom and His righteousness, and all these things will be given to you as well" (Matthew 6:33).

### Spiritual Values, Obligations and Benefits

Using the Sermon on the Mount as our starting point, we shall see that there is more to the Kingdom of God than being born again. As already explained, being born again is the first step in entering the Kingdom of God; it is an indispensable step in becoming a citizen of the Kingdom. But there is more: among other things, the citizens of the Kingdom of God in the second phase are expected to have clear priorities (See Matthew 6: 19-21; 33); they have spiritual values (as in the Beatitudes: Matthew 5:3-12); they have social obligations (Matthew 5:13-16); and they have benefits or privileges (Matthew 6:25-34). I elaborate on these below, citing examples from the Sermon on the Mount and other parts of the gospels.

### Priorities of the Citizens of the Kingdom

Jesus set priorities for the citizens of the Kingdom and identified spiritual values for them.

Top among the priorities is seeking the Kingdom of God: "But seek first His kingdom and His righteousness, and all these things will be given to you as well" (Matthew 6:33). The citizens must strive for the Kingdom and for righteousness. They must store up for themselves treasure in heaven "Where moths and vermin do not destroy, and where thieves do not break in and steal." Their hearts must be where their treasure is (Matthew 6:19-21).

They should guard against all kinds of greed, for "Life does not consist in an abundance of possessions" (Luke 12:15). They should not be like the rich fool who put all his effort into making arrangements for his harvest thinking that he would now "Take life easy, eat, drink and make merry," but God demanded his life just as he finished saying these words (Luke 12:13-21). Nor should they be like the rich man in the Parable of the Rich Man and Lazarus (See Luke 16:19-31); not even like the rich man who had kept all the commandments of God since he was a boy, but would not part with his possessions in order to follow Jesus (See Luke 18:18-29). They should rather take the example of the man who sold everything he had to buy the field with the hidden treasure, and the merchant who sold everything he had to buy a pearl of great value (See Matthew 13:44-46).

Making the Kingdom of God a top priority also means being prepared to suffer persecution. Now, persecution takes different forms: There was the persecution that Christians faced during the first few centuries when thousands and thousands of the followers of Jesus were martyred for the faith, just as in the 19th century, young Ugandan Christians were killed for becoming Christians. Even in the 21st century, some believers are facing persecution in countries where Christianity is not accepted as a religion.

But there are other forms of persecution in some so-called democratic countries. In such countries, followers of Jesus may find themselves being expected to do something that contradicts or violates their faith. As Jesus says, His disciples may be persecuted "Because of righteousness." He goes on to say "Blessed are you when people insult you, persecute you and falsely say all kinds of evil against you because of me" (Matthew 5:10-11). A principled person who points out the wrong things those in authority are doing, may be persecuted in the same way as prophets were persecuted by the leaders of the Jewish religion. In our time, there is a tendency to follow the standards of the world rather than the standards set by Jesus. By taking the Kingdom as their top priority, the citizens of the Kingdom should be prepared to face persecution in all these circumstances. This also means that the citizens of the Kingdom should be aware of the differences between the values set by Jesus and the values of the world in which they live.

### Spiritual Values

Among the spiritual values that Jesus taught His followers to be aware of and to cherish are the following included in the Beatitudes:
a) Being poor in spirit
b) Meekness
c) To hunger and thirst for righteousness
d) Being merciful
e) Being pure in heart
f) Acting as peacemakers.

The other two Beatitudes have to do with accepting situations in which they find themselves, mourning or being persecuted for righteousness (See Matthew 5:3-12; Luke 6:20-23).

# Jesus' Vision of The Kingdom of God on Earth

A spiritual value which is not articulated in the Beatitudes is striving to be perfect as the Father in heaven is perfect (See Matthew 5:48).

## *Social Obligations*

The citizens of the transitional phase of the Kingdom have a major leadership role in the world. Jesus came as the light of the world and He wanted His followers to play the role of light and salt in the world: "You are the salt of the earth... "You are the light of the world... In the same way, let your light shine before others, that they may see your good deeds and glorify your Father in heaven" (Matthew 5: 13-16).

This is one of the most important passages in the Sermon on the Mount, and indeed, in all the gospels. The followers of Jesus are not supposed to hide away from the world. They truly have a dual citizenship. They belong to the Kingdom of God, but they are also citizens of their respective natural states and of the world, and they have the same rights in these states as everyone else. They are not an "other worldly" group of people that only glorifies God by praying in secluded Churches. They are not *of* the world, but are *in* the world. Jesus clearly stated this in His prayer for His disciples just before He was arrested:

"My prayer is not that you take them out of the world... They are not of the world, even as I am not of it... As you sent me into the world, I have sent them into the world." (John 17:15-18). What are the implications of all this for the citizens of the kingdom?

Among other things, they should be actively involved in political affairs, social responsibilities, development programmes and other activities that support the betterment of society and the happiness of people. They should assist governments and other authorities where opportunities present themselves. Among the citizens of the Kingdom are specialists and experts in various spheres of human activity. This means playing a leadership role in fields such as education, health programmes, infrastructure development, the struggle against oppression and corruption etc. In terms of the Bible, the citizens of the Kingdom are, among other things, involved in humanitarian activities as explained in Matthew 25:31-40, meaning:

a) They feed the hungry and clothe the naked.
b) They welcome strangers in their homes.
c) They visit the sick in hospitals.
d) They visit prisoners.
e) They also perform works of mercy like the good Samaritan (See Luke 10:25-37).

These activities were prophesied by Isaiah as the kind of fasting that pleases the Lord:

"Is not this the kind of fasting I have chosen? To loose the chains of injustice and untie the cords of the yoke, to set the oppressed free and break every yoke? Is it not to share your food with the hungry and to provide the poor wanderer with shelter – when you see the naked, to clothe them, and not to turn away from your own flesh and blood... then your light will rise in the darkness, and your night will become like the noonday" (Isaiah 58:6-10).

# Jesus' Vision of The Kingdom of God on Earth

By being involved in works of mercy and fighting against all forms of oppression, poverty and deprivation, they truly become the light of the world. They work hard making use of the gifts and talents given to them as in the case of the Parable of Bags of Gold (See Matthew 25:14-30) and the Parable of the Ten Minas (See Luke 19:12-17). Each should examine the talents given to him or her and make effective use of them. Furthermore, they must remember they are branches of the true vine, who is Jesus. Any branch that does not bear fruit is cut off by the Father, who is the gardener. In order to bear fruit, each branch must remain in Jesus since no branch can bear fruit unless it remains in the vine. True disciples of Jesus remain in Jesus and bear much fruit, to the glory of God the Father (See John 15:1-8). True citizens of the Kingdom are therefore, exemplary in whatever they do, be it in the Church, or in social activities, or in the workplace. The citizenship of the Kingdom of God is not for lazybones. When you become a citizen, you become a disciple of Jesus, and that means hard work. It is not enough to be a pious individual who goes to Church every day. Your deeds in your community and the wider world are part of what makes you light and salt for fellow humans.

Jesus did not just preach the good news of the Kingdom – He also took care of people's material needs: He healed the sick; gave sight to the blind; and fed the hungry. In doing this, Jesus was fulfilling what had been prophesied about Him as exemplified by the passage from Isaiah quoted above. The glory of God and the essence of the Kingdom of God were revealed in the work He did and in how He conducted Himself. Similarly, citizens of the Kingdom of God work for the total liberation of humanity - including in the fight against diseases, poverty and social ills. When they walk in the footsteps of the Master like this, their light "will break forth like the dawn"; then their righteousness will go before them and the glory of the Lord will be their rear guard (See Isaiah 58:8). In whatever they do, they are not show-offs. They do not do these things in order to get praise from the public. Their aim is to work for the greater glory of God.

### Benefits and Rewards

Working for the Kingdom of God is hard work, but the advantages outstrip the difficulties encountered by those who commit themselves to the norms and requirements of the Kingdom. There are positive effects and outcomes in the Kingdom. I have divided the effects and outcomes into two categories: *benefits* and *rewards*. Benefits are those outcomes that flow naturally into the life of a loyal citizen or disciple of Jesus while they are here on earth during this transitional phase of the Kingdom of God; and rewards are the final outcomes in the third phase when the Church rules the world with Christ, and in the final phase when one is rewarded with eternal life. The rewards are also granted at the time one has left this world and his/her soul is taken to heaven.

### Benefits

The benefits of becoming a disciple of Jesus and working for the Kingdom of God are many, but I have identified the following:

a) Once they have sought the Kingdom and God's righteousness and made these their top priority, everything else they need will be given to them. We are not here necessarily talking about needs for money and good jobs. We are partly talking about what the Lord sees as important for them to be able to walk their journey as followers of Jesus in this difficult world.

b) Because they have surrendered themselves to God, they do not have to worry about anything, for God provides all their needs (See Matthew 6:25-34). What is more, they become people of peace for they will experience the amazing peace of Christ which enables them to face any tribulation without worry and anxiety. This is the peace Jesus promised His disciples when He said, "Peace I leave with you; my peace I give you. I do not give to you as the world gives" (John 14:28). It is the peace of God that Paul talks about "which transcends all understanding" (Philippians 4:7). Similarly, they do not have to be afraid of anything (See Luke 12:32). This is not to say they are not exposed to oppression and all other forms of suffering, but that their faith in God is such that they know He is with them wherever they go and whatever they do. They are therefore, conquerors in everything. As the Apostle Paul wrote, "No, in all these things we are more than conquerors through Him who loved us" (Romans 8:37). With such faith, they are able to gladly declare with the psalmist: "Even though I walk through the darkest valley, I will fear no evil, for you are with me; your rod and your staff, they comfort me" (Psalm 23:4).

c) When, as a group, they ask God for anything in the name of Jesus, it shall be given to them by God the

Father, because where two or three are gathered in His name, He will also be there to intercede for them (See Matthew 18:19-20).

d) As disciples of Jesus they are guided by the Spirit of truth, the Holy Spirit whom Jesus promised to send (See John 16:7-15). Through the Spirit, they receive power to be witnesses of Christ everywhere "to the ends of the earth" (Acts 1:8). They enjoy the benefit of living by the Spirit and receiving His seven-fold fruit: "Love, joy, peace, forbearance, kindness, goodness, faithfulness, gentleness and self-control" (Galatians 5:13-26). As individuals, they receive gifts to be used for the common good (See 1 Corinthians 12:1-11). The wisdom of God and things of God which those without the Spirit do not understand, and even consider foolishness, is revealed to them by the same Spirit (See 1 Corinthians 2: 6-16).

### *Rewards*

The rewards of the loyal citizens of the kingdom, the disciples of Jesus, can be summarised as follows:

a) By believing in Jesus and being born again, they will have eternal life (See John 3:15; 6:32-58).

b) Jesus will raise them up at the last day (See John 6:39, 44, 54).

c) They will be counted among the sheep of Jesus and inherit the kingdom of God at the end of the world (See Mathew 25:31-40).

d) Those who will be alive at the time of the great tribulation will be raptured and saved from the worst effects of that terrible period.

e) The dead among them at the time of Christ's second coming will be raised to life and rule the earth with Him for one thousand years (See Revelation 20:4-6).

f) They will see and live with God in the final and eternal phase of the Kingdom in the new heaven and the new earth. God will be their God and they will be His people, and He will wipe away every tear from their eyes (See Revelation 21: 1-4; 22: 1-5).

### *Jesus Brought News of a Kingdom of Life and Joy*

The above are some of the benefits and rewards of becoming citizens of the Kingdom that we should be informing the world about. There are advantages both in this world and in the world to come. In this world, followers of Jesus are not protected from problems and suffering, but their faith will give them the wisdom and capacity to cope with the difficulties of life. It was the strength they drew from this wisdom that enabled the apostles to rejoice when they were persecuted by the Jewish authorities for speaking in the name of Jesus: "The apostles left the Sanhedrin, rejoicing because they had been counted worthy of suffering disgrace for the Name" (Acts 5:41). Citizens of the Kingdom will also know that on the other side of the grave there is real life, for in death life is not ended but changed. They will have knowledge of these things revealed to them by the Holy Spirit. The Apostle Paul, quoting Isaiah, has commented: "'What no eye has seen, what no ear has heard, and what no human mind has conceived"- the things God has prepared for those who love him – these are the things God has revealed to us by his Spirit' (1 Corinthians 2:9-10).

Furthermore, this world as we know it will come to an end. However, citizens of the Kingdom know that at the end of time the earth will be transformed into something a lot more beautiful, a lot more enjoyable than all the beauty and material attractions of this fallen world. No doubt, those who are wise only in the things of this world, will think this is gibberish and subjective spiritual idealism and day dreaming. However, those who have been born again, those born of water and the Spirit, will be able to discern this wisdom of God that the Spirit reveals to those who believe in Jesus Christ as the Son of God and Saviour of the world. All this is part of the Good News that the citizens of the Kingdom of God should be conveying to the world. The problem of our present world is that we convey the news of the Kingdom in a manner that is not clear and convincing. We promise people heaven but in very vague terms. True, none of us have been to heaven and seen how things are there, but we do not articulate clearly those things that the Bible tells us. Furthermore, the message we give is that human life ends only in heaven; there is no understanding that this earth of ours will be recreated and we will have another and very enjoyable life here first, during the reign of Christ, and then at the end of the world, after the final judgment when *all things have been made new.*

### Jesus' Vision and Conditions for the Growth and Success of the Kingdom

So far, we have discussed the values citizens of the Kingdom must cherish and the obligations they must fulfil in order to enjoy the benefits and rewards we have summarised. But Jesus further had expectations that related, not only to benefits and rewards, but also to the growth and success of the Kingdom on earth. What does Jesus say about these? I will focus on four fundamental requirements that are based on Jesus' expectations. These are Faith, Hope, Love and Unity.

*Faith*

Faith is belief in God and in the One He sent to save the world from Satan and the sin of Adam. The faith we are required to have is something deeper than the Creed that many Christians recite on Sundays. It is to sincerely believe in Jesus as "The way and the truth and the life" (John 14:6). It is to believe that if we follow Him sincerely with real conviction, we can move mountains; we can facilitate the establishment of the Kingdom that Jesus hoped to see so that our world can reflect the values of the Kingdom of God more effectively.

When we look around us, we are dismayed by the extent to which the world is steeped in the values of the Kingdom of Satan. We are dismayed by the amount of suffering, the high levels of oppression and corruption; the frightening levels of immorality, cruelty and crime; the degree of injustice; the extent to which people worship power and wealth and the frightening speed at which secularism is spreading. Can the followers of Jesus really manage to be "the salt of the earth" and "the light of the world" in a world so deeply steeped in the values of the Kingdom of Satan? What we should remember though, is that it is not by our own power that we can change the world. It is God working through us; it is Jesus needing to continue His work through an army of believers.

The temptation is to just fold our hands and accept what is going on as inevitable in what some have described as a "post Christian age". We should however, remember Jesus' words:

77

# Learning to lead for the Kingdom

"Very truly I tell you, whoever believes in me will do the works I have been doing, and they will do even greater things than these, because I am going to the Father" (John 14:12). Jesus also told His disciples, "Truly, I tell you, if you have faith as small as a mustard seed, you can say to this mountain, 'Move from here to there,' and it will move" (Matthew 17:20). What we need is the faith of His mother Mary, who, on seeing that wine had run out at the wedding in Cana, simply said to Him, "They have no more wine"; and to the servants "Do whatever he tells you"; and indeed water was changed into wine (See John 2:1-11). What we need is to have the faith of the centurion, who was so convinced Jesus had the power to save his servant that he said, "Lord, don't trouble yourself, for I do not deserve to have You come under my roof… But say the word, and my servant will be healed" (Luke 7: 1-10; Matthew 8: 5-13). In our state of despair, we should be inspired by the faith of the woman who had been subjected to bleeding for twelve years under the care of many doctors, who said to herself, "If I just touch His clothes, I will be healed", and she was healed (See Mark 5: 21-34). We should have the faith of Abraham who, when Isaac asked "but where is the lamb for the burnt offering"? Abraham simply replied, "God Himself will provide the lamb for the burnt offering, my son" (Genesis 22:8).

Jesus expected his followers to behave like a people of faith in advancing the values of the Kingdom. Faced with the storms of life and the frightening wars raging against people of faith and the Kingdom of God in our time, we should cry out to the Lord like His disciples, who, in the face of a furious storm shouted, "Lord, save us! We're going to drown!" Then we should expect to hear His comforting voice, "You of little faith, why are you so afraid?" (Matthew 8:23-27). In our blindness that causes us to see only gloom and doom in our world, blindness that prevents us from reading the signs of a possible spiritual revival in the twenty-first century, we should, with the faith of the two blind men pray "Have mercy on us, Son of David!", and sincerely pray for the spiritual transformation of the world. We should hear the voice of Jesus saying, "According to your faith let it be done to you" (Matthew 9:27-29).

### Hope

Jesus had no illusion about the way the Kingdom of God was going to grow in the transitional phase. He knew Satan was going to be actively maintaining his hold on the world. Consequently, many would still be led astray even after He had died to save humanity. Hence, He gave the Parable of the Sower as an example of how the Kingdom was going to grow with some seed falling on rocky places, some among thorns etc, as was explained in the previous chapter (See Mark 4:1-20). Similarly, in the Parable of the Weeds (See Matthew 13:24-30), the man sows good seed, but the enemy comes and sows weeds among the wheat. The man tells his servants "Let both grow together until the harvest." At harvest time, the weeds are collected first and burned; and then the wheat is collected into the barn. In His interpretation of the Parable (Matthew 13:36-43), Jesus explains plainly: the man who sowed good seed is the Son of Man, the field is the world, the good seed are the people of the Kingdom, the weeds are the people of the evil one, the enemy is the devil, the harvesters are angels and the harvest is "the end of the age", meaning the end of this transitional phase, before Christ's second coming. This Parable reads just like another version of "the sheep" and "the goats" at the end of time (See Mathew 25:31-46).

However, Jesus was very optimistic about the growth of the Kingdom of God in the transitional phase despite the impediments caused by the work of the devil and the people of the evil Kingdom. He gave the example of the Parable of the Mustard Seed and the Parable of Yeast, both of which we have explained. He also gave the example of the Growing Seed (Mark 4:26-29). A man scatters seed on the ground. "Night and day, whether he sleeps or gets up, the seed sprouts and grows, though he does not know how. All by itself the soil produces grain…" These three parables give a very optimistic view of the growth of the Kingdom of God in our time.

After His resurrection, Jesus was no longer speaking in parables, but in plain language that left His disciples with no doubt about how optimistic He was about the success of His mission on earth. This optimism comes through in the Great Commission: "All authority in heaven and on earth has been given to me. Therefore, go and make disciples of all nations, baptizing them in the name of the Father and of the Son and of the Holy Spirit, and teaching them to obey everything I have commanded you. And surely I am with you always, to the very end of the age" (Matthew 28:18-20).

In Mark's Gospel, He is quoted as having said, "Go into all the world and preach the gospel to all creation" (Mark 16:15). The gospel and values of the Kingdom should be so powerfully communicated that they permeate the times. This will be evident during the millennium when there is harmony between humanity and other living things.

# Jesus' Vision of The Kingdom of God on Earth

In the Acts of the Apostles, Luke quotes the disciples asking, "Lord, are you at this time going to restore the Kingdom to Israel?" They were still thinking in terms of the political Kingdom the Jews expected the Messiah to bring. His response drew their attention to a spiritual and universal Kingdom, and was an emphatic expression of His optimism: "It is not for you to know the times or dates the Father has set by his own authority. But you will receive power when the Holy Spirit comes on you; and you will be my witnesses in Jerusalem, and in all Judea and Samaria, and to the ends of the earth" (Acts 1:6-8). The followers of Jesus must be people of hope, but hope that is strengthened by their active work for the Kingdom.

## Love

Love is a key feature of Jesus' mission and He regarded it as one of the fundamental dimensions of the Kingdom of God. His coming on earth was an expression of God's love for the children of Adam and Eve, who had lost the kingdom as a consequence of their parents' disobedience. His death on the cross was the highest expression of love for humankind. The evangelist tells us, "For God so loved the world that he gave his one and only Son, that whoever believes in him shall not perish but have eternal life" (John 3:16). By betraying the Lord, we humans had acted like the Lost Son (See Luke 15:11-32); we had rejected His "sonship" to use Paul's term, but the Lord felt such love and compassion for us that at our redemption by the sacrifices of His own Son He was happy "to throw his arms around us and kiss us" (vs 20) because we had been lost but were found (vs 32).

81

# Learning to lead for the Kingdom

But because God loved us so much, we also need to reflect this love to God, to others and to one another. Jesus made it clear He came to fulfil, not to abolish the Law (See Matthew 5:17-20). When a Pharisee who was an expert of the Law asked Him which was the greatest commandment in the Law, Jesus answered: "'Love the Lord your God with all your heart and with all your soul and with all your mind.' This is the first and greatest commandment. And the second is like it: 'Love your neighbour as yourself'. All the Law and the Prophets hang on these two commandments" (Matthew 22:34-40; Mark 12:28-31). Developing from this, in order to fulfil the Law, Jesus adds a third dimension. In the Kingdom that He was preaching, people should not only love God and neighbour as stated in the Law; they should also love one another. This feature of the Kingdom was so important that it was by this very fact of loving one another that the world would know as a unique and distinctive characteristic of his followers: "A new command I give you: Love one another. As I have loved you, so you must love one another. By this everyone will know that you are my disciples, if you love one another" (John 13:34). If there was anything that was to act as a trademark of the followers of Jesus as a group, it was that they loved one another.

Jesus repeats this exhortation in chapter 15 where He draws attention to the need for His followers to keep His commands so that they can remain in His love just as He has kept the Father's commands and remains in His love (See John 15:9-17). This theme is so important we shall return to it later.

# Jesus' Vision of The Kingdom of God on Earth

## *Unity*

The fourth element that is crucial for the success of the Kingdom of God during its second phase is unity – the unity of Jesus' followers. He did not comment much about this when He was still with His disciples, but it features in one of His most passionate prayers just before His arrest. One of the saddest things about Christianity is how badly divided the people who call themselves followers of Jesus are. More and more sects are coming into being, and one wonders where the splitting process will end. The sad thing is, Jesus actually referred to the unity of Christians as a feature by which the world would know that He had been sent by the Father. It is as if He had foreseen how hopelessly divided His followers would be in our time when He was prompted to say this prayer which is not quoted in full here:

"My prayer is not for them alone. I pray also for those who will believe in me through their message, that all of them may be one, Father, just as you are in me and I am in you. May they also be in us so that the world may believe that you have sent me. I have given them the glory that you gave me, that they may be one as we are one – I in them and you in me – so that they may be brought to complete unity. Then, the world will know that you sent me..." (John 17:20-23).

There was a time in the 20$^{th}$ century when ecumenism appeared to be a movement that was going to respond effectively to Jesus' prayer, but the fire seems to have died down. We are quite happy worshipping God in our separate churches. Some seem to think the Holy Spirit will do the work for us while we sit back and glory in our separate denominations. Let us ask to be empowered by the Holy Spirit to do the work that Jesus wants us to do, but let us not behave as if we are delegating the Holy Spirit to perform our duties. This is another theme we shall return to later as it says much about how the followers of Jesus should relate to one another and to the world.

### The Lord's Prayer and the Kingdom of God

A major reference point in our efforts to work for the Kingdom of God and to understand Jesus' conception of it is the Lord's Prayer, the "Our Father." One gets the impression that all too often we are just mouthing the words "Thy kingdom come/Thy will be done on earth as it is in heaven" without paying attention to what they are intended to signify. On the contrary, these are words that should give us a sense of purpose, a sense of mission. It is therefore, necessary to unpack the meaning and significance of the prayer.

### Praying for the Reign of Christ

In teaching this prayer, Jesus was in part telling us how important the coming of the Kingdom of God should be in our faith. As already explained, there are two major dimensions of God's Kingdom on earth, two phases of the Kingdom that are of concern to us. First, there is the actual Kingdom of God on earth when God is in charge on this earth – that is the reign of Christ. As noted in Chapter 1, Albert Nolan (1992:83, 84) explains that the Greek word *basileia* which has been translated in English as "Kingdom" means "kingship" or "royal power". When we pray for God's Kingdom to come on earth and for His will to be done on earth as it is in heaven, we are yearning for this time of God's political power to come to our world. This is what we have characterised as the *Third Phase* of the Kingdom of God on earth. It is the time when Jesus, Our Lord and Master, is ruling as King on this earth and those of us who will have been resurrected will be ruling with Him (See Revelation 20:4-6). We have already briefly described in Chapter 2 what a utopia this earth will be under the leadership of Christ, when there is absolute peace and harmony between all human beings and other living creatures; when justice prevails; when the King Himself is a Counsellor and a Shepherd; when those who rule with Christ will be servants of the people and not dictators; when the Israelites are back in their own land and have accepted Jesus as their Messiah... It is a wonderful world, and this is the world the early Christians were looking forward to. They were eager to see Jesus returning as King; hence, they prayed *Maranatha!* "Come, Lord!" (1 Corinthians 16:22). The early Christians understood, as we should, that Jesus wanted His followers to be eager for His reign to come, and consequently to pray for its coming.

As we pray for the coming of the reign of Christ, the millennium, we should not be forgetful of the tribulation that precedes it. We should always be conscious of the warning that Our Lord and Master gives us about the end times in the gospels: Matthew 24: 1-51; Mark 13:1-37; and Luke 17: 20-37 and 21:5-36. There are two key lessons that Jesus teaches us about the end times: First, that we do not know when it will be; and second, that we should always be ready. A key point to remember here, is that should the tribulation occur in our life, we should pray to the Lord that we be raptured with His elect and escape its terrible effects.

# Learning to lead for the Kingdom

*Praying for the Values of the Kingdom to Permeate our Present World*

Our second aim in saying "Thy kingdom come" should be for the values of the Kingdom to permeate the present phase – the second or transitional phase of the Kingdom. Every time we say "Thy kingdom come" we should be reminded about how much work there is still to be done in spreading the gospel and the values of the Kingdom of God in our time. These words should remind us of our Lord saying to His disciples, "The harvest is plentiful but the workers are few" (Matthew 9:37). Jesus said these words after He had seen suffering crowds of people and had compassion on them "Because they were harassed and helpless, like sheep without a shepherd" (Matthew 9:36). The scene that moved Jesus to compassion then is still all too familiar in our cities, towns and villages, where people suffer from hunger, starvation, oppression, disease, and lack of spiritual wholeness, among other problems. We should consequently, "Ask the Lord of the harvest, therefore, to send out workers into his harvest field" (Matthew 9:38). We need politicians, social workers, health workers and religious leaders who have enough compassion to work for the improvement of people's material and spiritual lives. We need to pray for our world to be a world in which God is real; in which the haves feel for, and willingly come to the aid of, the have-nots; in which people are conscious of the need to conduct themselves in ways that are consistent with the values that Jesus came to impart. The rapid spread of secularism in our time is an indication of the extent to which humanity has lost hope in all religions and in the purpose of life in this world. The Lord's Prayer should motivate us to be a purpose driven people because we know what the purpose of life is in this life and in the next, and we want other people to understand that purpose. We know the glorious and utopian nature of the reign of Christ, and we want the world to be aware of it.

Jesus expects us to heed the message of the Parable of the Ten Minas (See Luke 19:11-16). In terms of this, the citizens of the Kingdom have major responsibilities in promoting the message and values of the Kingdom; in promoting justice and peace; in struggling for the creation of a more egalitarian society; in alleviating poverty; in fighting diseases; and in promoting among ourselves the virtues of faith, hope, love and Christian unity, among other things. We cannot all do everything that has to be done. Consequently, each should examine themselves to see and understand the gifts they have been given and the responsibilities that go with those gifts. Each should ask, "What is my role in advancing the cause of the Kingdom?"

The man of noble birth in the parable said to his servants, "Put this money to work until I come back" (Luke 19:13 NIV). In the New Jerusalem Bible (Luke 19:13 NJB) he says, "Trade with these until I come back". And in the New Revised Standard Version (Luke 19:13 NRSV) he says, "Do business with these until I come back". From all these translations it becomes clear that Jesus expects hard work from His disciples. He does not want us to just pray for our own Salvation; but wants us to actively make use of the talents we have been given to further the Kingdom of God; to facilitate the coming of the Kingdom on earth; and to hasten the time when the will of God is "done on earth as it is in heaven." Work in the Church should not be business as usual; it should be "business unusual." If we actively join forces in advancing the cause of the Kingdom, we will be like an army fighting for the victory of the kingdom of God in its perpetual struggle with the Kingdom of Satan. Ron Boehme (1989:153) puts it this way, "Jesus does not want us to retreat from the world, but to occupy it – possess it and rule it – just as an occupying army would." We should occupy the world with the gospel message of Jesus in preparation for the millennium when He comes to rule the world as King.

### The Kingdom of God within Us

But there is something we should remember: When we say, "Thy kingdom come /Thy will be done on earth as it is in heaven", we might easily forget to include ourselves in those we want to do the will of God. In *Come, Follow Me*, I made a distinction between what I called *The Kingdom of God within us* and *the Kingdom of God around us*. 'The former has to do with our personal spiritual condition, our own spiritual being in relation to the values of God..." (Ngara 2001:7 ff). One condition for facilitating the coming of the Kingdom in the second phase is to strive to reflect the Kingdom in all we do, think and say. People should see the values of the Kingdom reflected in us, just as Jesus reflected the Kingdom in His words, actions and character. Similarly, we should ourselves strive to do the will of God here on earth as it is done in heaven. Jesus brought the Kingdom wherever He went; we should not only preach the Kingdom, but take the Kingdom wherever we go.

# Jesus' Vision of The Kingdom of God on Earth

## *The Picture that Emerges - Relationships in the Transitional Phase of the Kingdom*

How can one attempt to characterize the vision of the Kingdom that Jesus could have had, judging by what He said and did? One should state from the outset that the analysis done in this chapter, is by no means a complete account of what Jesus said and did. It would therefore, be presumptuous to suggest the account given in this chapter serves as an adequate basis for proposing a summary of Jesus' vision or conception of the Kingdom of God in our time. For one thing, the account given in this chapter, does not cover some of Jesus' important teachings. For example, we have not touched on the significance of some key parables like the Parable of the Good Samaritan and the Parables of the Lost Son and the Lost Sheep. What is more, we have so far not referred to His pronouncements on leadership which is one of the principal issues we must discuss in this book.

However, the analysis we have done so far, enables us to identify some key features of Jesus' portrayal of the Kingdom of God. The following are some of the features: First, the Kingdom that Jesus came to proclaim was open to anyone who chose to enter, but there were conditions one had to fulfil. The first condition was to believe in the Son of Man, "For God so loved the world that he gave his one and only Son, that whoever believes in him shall not perish but have eternal life" (John 3:16). An important feature is to see the vision in terms of a whole system of relationships: At one level, the individual follower of Jesus must think of his/her relationship with God or the Trinity, with Jesus, with neighbours, with one's enemies. At another level, you have the citizens of the Kingdom, the

89

followers of Jesus, as a community and a collective: How they relate to one another, to Jesus and to the world? Finally, there is the relationship between God and His people.

### The Individual and God (the Trinity)

For the individual disciple of Jesus, there would be a radically new way of relating to God and to others, and a completely new way of understanding what is valuable in life. In regard to his/her relationship with God, the disciple would have to understand the Kingdom comes first – above everything else; above all human needs. Hence, "But seek first his kingdom and his righteousness." That is priority number one. As for all the things of life, whatever they may be, "and all these things will be given to you as well" (Matthew 6:33). The individual had to understand that seeking the Kingdom entailed having a righteous relationship with God, which meant being repentant, undergoing an internal transformation such that one was not guilty before God. It would mean being sincere without any pretences or hypocrisy, without any public show of one's piety, so much so that prayer would be in one's secret room, with a closed door (See Matthew 6:5-6).

Such a disciple, would not be like some who pretentiously mouth the words "Lord, Lord" without doing the will of the Father in heaven (See Matthew 7:21 -23). For the true disciple, the true citizen of the Kingdom, the Kingdom of God would be like a hidden treasure or a pearl of great value for which one would be prepared to sell everything in order to buy it (See Matthew 13:44-46).

# Jesus' Vision of The Kingdom of God on Earth

Thus this would entail such total surrender to God that one would see no need to even worry about anything (See Matthew 6:25-34). As Jesus came to fulfil the Law, this requirement for His disciples would be in fulfilment of the greatest commandment: "Love the LORD your God with all your heart and with all your soul and with all your strength" (Deuteronomy 6:5). In this way, the disciples' righteousness would surpass that of the Pharisees and Teachers of the Law (See Matthew 5: 17-20).

### The Individual and Jesus

The individual disciple's fruitful relationship with God and with others, would depend on his/her relationship with Jesus. It is by believing in Jesus; being born of water and the Spirit that the believer will gain the right to enter the Kingdom of heaven (See John 3: 1-16). While still in this transitional phase of the Kingdom, the disciple would be required to bear fruit by way of spreading the message and values of the Kingdom of God. But to be able to bear fruit, the disciple would need to remain in Jesus, to be a branch of the vine that bears fruit by remaining in the vine (See John 15: 1-8). To remain in Jesus and be able to bear fruit and gain eternal life, the disciple would have to keep Jesus' commands (See John 15: 9-17) and eat His body and drink His blood (See John 6: 26-59). Keeping Jesus' commands would mean obeying Him in the same way that He obeyed the Father while He was here on earth. Remaining in Jesus would mean following Him as "the way and the truth and the life" (John 14:6), and working hard to continue the Saviour's mission of spreading the Good News of the Kingdom of God. It would also entail following Jesus through thick and thin, heeding the Messiah's injunction, "Whoever does not take up their cross and follow me is not worthy of me" (Matthew 10:38).

### The Disciple's Relationship to Others

As already indicated, following the values of the Kingdom as taught by Jesus, would entail a radically new way of relating to other people. First, there would be how one relates to one's neighbour. In the Law of Moses, your neighbour was a fellow Israelite, for it was written: "Do not do anything that endangers your neighbour's life... Do not hate a fellow Israelite in your heart... Do not seek revenge or bear a grudge against anyone among your people, but love your neighbour as yourself" (Leviticus 19:16-18).

In the transitional phase of the Kingdom, it was not going to be enough to love fellow Israelites. Your neighbours included your enemies and you even had to pray for those who persecute you. In this way, Jesus' disciple would be like his/her Father in heaven: "He causes His sun to rise on the evil and the good, and sends rain on the righteous and the unrighteous." The love of the citizens of the Kingdom had to surpass that of the tax collectors and pagans. (See Matthew 5:43-48). Furthermore, loving one's neighbour also meant coming to the assistance of anyone who needed one's help as was demonstrated by the Good Samaritan who took pity on the man attacked by robbers, bandaged his wounds, took him to an inn to have him taken care of at the Samaritan's own expense (See Luke 10:25-37). In matters of love of neighbour, the disciple of Jesus had to aspire to be perfect as the Father in heaven is perfect (See Matthew 5:48). Loving your neighbour entailed being merciful; and what the Good Samaritan did was an example of being merciful as the Father in heaven is merciful (See Luke 6:36).

But more was demanded of the disciple of Jesus in terms of relationships with others. It entailed not taking revenge, and agreeing to lend those who want to borrow from one (See Matthew 5:38-42). It entailed avoiding to judge others (See Matthew 7:1-5). The bottom line to one's relationship with others, or the basic guideline was to be this: "So in everything, do to others what you would have them do to you, for this sums up the Law and the Prophets" (Matthew 7:12; Lk 6:31).

### The Community of Disciples of Jesus

The community of Jesus' disciples would love one another. Theirs would be a society that would be known as a people who love one another as the Lord commanded. This requirement was fulfilled by the early Christians about whom it is said people would comment, "See how these Christians love one another." Sadly, this cannot be said about Jesus' followers in our time; but it is a reminder to twenty-first century Christians that not only does the Lord expect it, but that it has actually been practiced by the prototype disciples of Jesus, and is therefore, possible.

The fact that the love of the early Christians for one another was noticed by those who did not belong to the faith, is an indication that these early citizens of the transitional phase lived up to one of the most important characteristic of the followers of Jesus – they were *in* this world, but not *of* this world. This is a key requirement. The community of followers of Jesus must be actively involved in the affairs of their respective natural countries, but guided by the principles and values of the Kingdom of God as has already been explained.

In view of the above, the community of disciples of Jesus would not only be expected to be *in* the world, but to be active participants who play a leading role in shaping the world. They were to be "the light of the world" and "the salt of the earth." Any idea that they would just practice their piety quietly and watch the world going astray would be a betrayal of the mission of Jesus because as salt, they would have lost their saltiness. And what was to be done to such salt? "It is no longer good for anything, except to be thrown out and trampled underfoot" (Matthew 5:13). The citizens of the transitional phase of the Kingdom would be expected to impact the world in two principal ways: First, they have the duty to work for the extension of the Kingdom so that all nations and all peoples of the world would come to know Christ and His message. Second, they were to fight to make the world a more just, more equal, more merciful and more caring world. In other words, the goal is to impact the world in such a way that it becomes more and more something of a mirror of the Kingdom of God during the reign of Christ. Just as humankind was made in the image of God, the earth itself resembles heaven in some way, so, Christians should work for the social fabric of humankind to be something of a mirror of the Kingdom of God in heaven.

### The Church and the Kingdom of God

*The Church and the Kingdom*

An important relationship that should be discussed, is between the Christian Church and the kingdom of God. Can we identify the Kingdom with the Church? Does being a member of the Church mean being a citizen of the Kingdom? We begin with two quotes:

# Jesus' Vision of The Kingdom of God on Earth

A. "Blessed are you, Simon son of Jonah, for this was not revealed to you by flesh and blood, but by my Father in heaven. And I tell you that you are Peter, and on this rock I will build my Church, and the gates of Hades will not overcome it. I will give you the keys of heaven; whatever you bind on earth will be bound in heaven, and whatever you loose on earth will be loosed in heaven" (Matthew 16:17-19).

B. "The coming of the kingdom of God is not something that can be observed, nor will people say, 'Here it is,' or 'There it is,' because the kingdom of God is in your midst" (Luke 17:20-21).

Is Jesus referring to the same entity in these two passages? Can we say the Kingdom of God that Jesus, responding to the Pharisees, said was "in your midst" referred to the Church that he was yet to build? As was discussed in the previous chapter, some authorities identify the Christian Church with the Kingdom of God, suggesting the Church is the Kingdom of God which needs to be purified. On his part, Albert Nolan says the Kingdom of God is a political notion, "A politically structured society of people here on earth" (Nolan, 1992:59). About the Church he says, "Jesus cannot be fully identified with that great religious phenomenon of the Western world known as Christianity" (Nolan, 1995). For this writer, the Kingdom of God and the Christian Church are closely related but not the same. For one thing, the Church is something that can be observed. People can actually say, "There is the Christian Church." As discussed earlier, the Kingdom of God on our present earth can be seen to have three phases: the original Kingdom in Eden, the Kingdom of God in the second or transitional phase after Christ's first coming, and the third phase or the millennium when Christ is ruling this world as King. The third phase will be followed by eternity in the new heaven and the new earth. In this regard, we have defined the Kingdom of God in the transitional phase as "A society or an ideal state in which people live according to the standards set by Jesus." The Holy City of Jerusalem has been examined in some detail in Chapter 2, where we came to a convincing conclusion that the new Jerusalem is a fusion of the Church of Jesus Christ and the faith of the twelve tribes of Israel, meaning that the new Jerusalem is founded on the truth of God as revealed in both the Old Testament and the New Testament – with Jesus Christ as the Bridegroom or Redeemer of members of both covenants. Our task in this part of this chapter, is to interrogate whether the Christian Church of the second phase should be conceived as having the same identity as the Kingdom of God.

Strong arguments for identifying the Church with the New Jerusalem of the New Earth could be based on Ephesians 5:23-33 and Colossians 1:22. As in a number of Paul's letters, such as 1 Corinthians 12, and similarly in Ephesians 5:23, the Church is referred to as "the body of Christ", a concept generally accepted and used by all Christians. Now, there are very strong echoes of Revelation 21 and 22 in Ephesians 5:23-33 and Colossians 1:22. It is best to put these Scripture passages side by side as shown below:

1. "For the husband is the head of the wife as Christ is the head of the church, his body, for which he is the Saviour... Husbands, love your wives, just as Christ loved the church and gave himself up for her to make her holy, cleansing her by the washing with water through the word, and to present her to himself as a radiant church without stain or wrinkle or any other blemish, but holy and blameless." (Ephesians 5:23-27).

2. But now he has reconciled you by Christ's physical body through death to present you holy in his sight, without blemish and free from accusations – if you continue in your faith, established and firm, and do not move from the hope held out in the gospel." (Colossians 1:22).

3. I saw the Holy City, the new Jerusalem, coming down out of heaven from God, prepared as a bride beautifully dressed for her husband."(Revelation 21:2 ).

4. 'One of the seven angels ... came and said to me, "Come, I will show you the bride, the wife of the Lamb. And he carried me away in the Spirit to a mountain great and high, and showed me the Holy City, Jerusalem, coming down out of heaven from God ..."'(Revelation 21:9-10).

A close scrutiny of these Scripture passages can, with good reason, lead the reader to associate the Church in the first two with the new Jerusalem in the second two, leading to the conclusion that the bride, "the wife of the Lamb" is the Christian Church. This is a matter that has been already settled in Chapter 2. In the first two passages quoted above, Paul presents an ideal picture of the Church, and no doubt, we all look forward to a time when the Church will be as pure as Paul presents it, but as argued elsewhere in this book, and implied in Albert Nolan's comment cited above, the Church as an institution has too many blemishes to deserve to be identified with the Kingdom of God preached by Jesus Christ.

Paul himself admits the blemishes in some of his writings, e.g. 1 Corinthians 3:1-5; 5:1-3. A closer look at Colossians 1:22, reveals a further problem in identifying the Church with the Kingdom. Paul adds a qualification to what he says to the Colossians: They will be presented holy in God's sight and without blemish and free from accusations "*If you continue in*

# Learning to lead for the Kingdom

*your faith, established and firm, and do not move from the hope held out in the gospel.*" Can we honestly say the institutional Church – in its various denominations – has met the requirements set by Paul? The pure Church that we would like to see in the second phase of the Kingdom, does not just emerge from nowhere. We have to work hard towards that ideal, as will be discussed later in the book.

That the Church has a key role in the establishment of God's Kingdom on earth cannot be doubted by disciples of Jesus or the group we have designated as "the citizens of the Kingdom." As a leader, Jesus knew that it was not enough to preach the Kingdom of God to an amorphous group of people. There had to be a structure and there had to be leaders. Accordingly, He trained the leaders and sent the Holy Spirit on the day of Pentecost to empower the Apostles so that they could become His witnesses and boldly proclaim the Kingdom, and on that day the Church was born (See Acts 2:1-41). The Lord then called Paul to be the Apostle of the Gentiles, and Paul laid the foundations of Christian missionary work and Christian theology. The early Christians were such ardent and faithful witnesses of Jesus that the mighty Roman Empire was eventually converted to the Christian faith. Christians appeared to others to be a wonderful community, and one of their remarkable characteristics was that they loved one another so much that people remarked, "See how these Christians love one another."

The Christian Church has done much to advance the Kingdom of God: For example, it has given us the Bible; it administers the sacraments; has played a major role in promoting education; and has taken the message of Christ to all parts of the world. In this regard, the Church can be taken as a vehicle for the promotion and advancement of the Kingdom of God in the world. But before we proceed on this point, we should perhaps pause briefly and reflect on the two

# Jesus' Vision of The Kingdom of God on Earth

Gospel passages marked A and B above. Jesus did not say, "On this rock I will build God's Kingdom"; He said "And on this rock I will build my church, and the gates of Hades will not overcome it." Very importantly, He went on to say, "I will give you the keys of heaven." This is the translation of the New International Version (NIV). In both the New Jerusalem Bible (NJB) and the New Revised Standard Version (NRSV) Jesus is quoted as having said, "I will give you the keys of the kingdom of heaven." This makes the relationship between the kingdom of God and the church clear. Through Peter, the church holds the keys to the Kingdom. Consequently, in this transitional phase of the Kingdom, the church is an agent that Jesus uses to take people to the Kingdom of God. This is not the Kingdom itself: rather, it is the boat, bus or aeroplane to the Kingdom. As we saw in the previous chapter, the new Jerusalem where the centre of the Kingdom will be, will be built on a combination of the Church of Jesus Christ and the Jerusalem of the twelve tribes of Israel.

At this juncture, it is useful to stop briefly and ponder what Jesus meant when He said, "Because the Kingdom of God is in your midst." In the New Jerusalem Bible, the translation says, "For, look, the Kingdom of God is among you." In the New Revised Standard Version, the translation is, "For, in fact, the kingdom of God is among you." This seems to be a puzzling response to the question asked by the Pharisees. One understands it better when one remembers the Pharisees and Teachers of the Law were fond of asking for a sign to show that Jesus was the Messiah. They were also looking to the time of the Messiah who would liberate them from Roman domination. Jesus' answer was that they should recognise the Kingdom in the work He did in healing the poor, the sick and the blind and in the miracles He was performing. He was the Messiah who represented the Kingdom that He preached about. Where He was, there was the Kingdom also.

# Learning to lead for the Kingdom

This answer was similar to the one He gave to Philip when the disciple asked Him, "Lord, show us the Father and that will be enough for us." He answered, "Don't you know me Philip, even after I have been among you for such a long time? Anyone who has seen me has seen the Father..." (John 14:8-9 ff). Similarly, anyone who had seen Him, heard what He said and saw what He did, had come in contact with the Kingdom of God.

## *Concluding Comments on Jesus' Vision of the Kingdom*

In trying to understand Jesus' vision of the Kingdom of God, we have covered a fairly vast terrain, which by itself by no means gives what can be called a full and comprehensive portrayal of the Saviour's vision. This is a very brief summary of the terrain covered. The features we noted include the following:

First, Jesus came to restore the Kingdom humankind had lost when Adam and Eve disobeyed God. In restoring the Kingdom, He would be fulfilling the Law and the Prophets. This restoration, He would do by bringing a new standard, a new way of looking at the relationship between God and human beings; the relationship between person and person; and of understanding what is valuable in life, and how one should conduct oneself in all situations. The yardstick of the followers of Jesus in behaviour and in all things would be to be holy and perfect people: "Be perfect, therefore, as your heavenly Father is perfect." (Matthew 5:48). In this way His followers would be *in* the world but not *of* the world, and would in that regard have dual citizenship status, as they would be both citizens of their natural states, but also citizens of a supernatural state of the Kingdom of God whose standards are set by Jesus. The first requirement of this citizenship, would be to belief in Jesus as the Saviour of the world and to be born again of water and the Spirit. This would be the qualification for entering the Kingdom of God when one leaves this world.

During the transitional phase on earth, the Kingdom of God would be growing in an environment that is dominated by the values of the Kingdom of Satan. The followers of Jesus would need to know there is a perpetual struggle between Good and Evil, and that they are part of Jesus' army in this struggle for souls. Now, in order to spread the Good News of the Kingdom of God in a coherent and systematic way, Jesus was going to establish the Church and, through Peter, its first Head, give it the keys of the Kingdom of heaven. Through the Church, the followers would be responsible for preaching the Good News to all nations – "to the ends of the earth." To be effective messengers of the Kingdom, the followers would have to obey Jesus' commands and remain in Him as He would be the vine and they its branches. For Him to win the human race back to the Kingdom of God, Jesus Himself would be the sacrificial Lamb whose blood would be shed for humanity. On their part, the followers would have to be prepared to suffer and be persecuted, and even to lose their lives for the Kingdom. The motto that would guide them would be: "But seek first his kingdom and his righteousness, and all these things will be given to you as well." (Matthew 6:33).

Part of the vision was that the end times could come any time, and the citizens of the Kingdom would have to adopt a double strategy – of keeping watch for the day of the Lord, but at the same time proceeding with the mission of evangelising the world. The details of the end times come to us from what Jesus Himself tells us in the gospels, supplemented by information we get from the Book of Revelation and the letters of the apostles Paul and Peter. The information can be summarised as follows: There will be a great catastrophe or great tribulation, in other words, "great distress" totally unequalled throughout human history, after which the sun and moon will be darkened and the stars will fall from heaven. Immediately prior to "the great distress", Jesus will send His angels with a loud trumpet call to gather the elect from every part of the earth. This will be "the rapture of the church" when faithful followers of Jesus will be flown out of the world to escape the distress. (See Matthew 24:15-31; 1 Thessalonians 4: 16-17). The dead will rise from the dead; and the living elect will be caught up together with the risen saints in the clouds to be with the Lord from then on.

Following this, Jesus returns to the world at this, His Second Coming, as a conquering Warrior and King. Israel will recognize Jesus Christ as the Messiah when He comes back this time, because this time He will be saving the Jewish nation from the threat of annihilation by the Anti-Christ and his allies. His enemies, the Anti-Christ and the false prophet, will be killed together with their armies, while their leader, Satan, will be imprisoned in the Abyss for one thousand years, when Christ and His saints will be ruling the world. As the Saviour of Jerusalem and Israel, Jesus will this time fulfil the Jewish conception of the Messiah. Israel will consequently repent and recognise Jesus as its King during the millennium – the thousand years during which Jesus will be ruling the world with His saints, while Satan is imprisoned. At the end of the millennium, Satan will be released from prison for a short while, and He will once again try to rally the world against Jesus; but he will be thrown into the lake of burning sulphur, where he will join the beast (the Anti-Christ) and the false prophet, and where they will burn for ever and ever.

Christ will sit in judgement to reward everyone for what they have done while in this world. Those who are not found in the book of life, will be thrown into the lake of burning fire where they will join Satan, the beast and the false prophet. To those whose names will be found in the book of life, Christ will say, "Come, you who are blessed by my Father; take your inheritance, the Kingdom prepared for you since the creation of the world" (Matthew 25:34). It is at this stage, "after He has destroyed all dominion, authority and power" that Jesus will hand over the Kingdom to God the Father (See 1 Corinthians 15:24). The stage should then be set for the glorious Wedding Supper of the Lamb. The new Jerusalem will be the Bride, and Jesus the triumphant Bridegroom. The invitees will be all the saved, all the elect, from both the Old Covenant and the New Covenant whom Christ will have fashioned into one nation. The redeemed will live joyfully forever in the New Heaven and the New Earth and will see God face-to-face.

Before we conclude, it is necessary to point out that for Jesus' disciples to proclaim the Kingdom effectively, they need to lead like Jesus. Consequently, they need to know Jesus' leadership style, and to understand His teaching on leadership. This is a topic that was not included in our discussion of Jesus' vision of the kingdom. It is such an important topic that the next two chapters are devoted to Jesus' leadership practice and His teaching on leadership for the Kingdom.

Learning to lead for the Kingdom

# CHAPTER FOUR

## Foundations of Kingdom Leadership Principles

*The Need for a New Understanding of Kingdom Leadership*

Dr Myles Munroe (2006:20) argues that Christianity as a religion is well known, studied and researched, "but little or nothing is known about the Kingdom." He goes on to say, as already indicated, "The result is that few so-called ordained ministers and priests have any formal instruction at all in any Kingdom concept." Another weakness down the ages has been to neglect, if not ignore, Jesus' teaching on leadership. Not many priests, pastors and religious sisters have been trained in leadership, and many do not seem to be aware of Jesus' approach to leadership, and consequently, many do not lead as Jesus would want them to.

The time has come for the disciples of Jesus to show they do not just follow a religion, but are citizens of the Kingdom of God who want to attract the people of the world to that Kingdom. The time has come for the disciples of Jesus to mean what they say, when they pray "Thy kingdom come / Thy will be done on earth as it is in heaven." The time has come for the followers of Jesus to actively work and pray for the coming of the Kingdom. For this to happen, we need to have a cadre of

# Learning to lead for the Kingdom

leaders who are imbued with the spirit of the Kingdom and are capable of guiding and leading others to the Kingdom. We need to have a cadre of leaders who understand and practice Jesus' approach to leadership. It is my hope that this book will be able to assist in this development. To this end, we shall now proceed to examine the principles and characteristics of Kingdom leadership.

### Common Basic Leadership Principles

The basic principles of leadership are the same regardless of faith, religion, ideology or type of organisation. To be an effective leader, one must understand what leadership is and what it is not. For instance, one must understand the difference between leadership and management. The necessary qualities of a leader such as having a vision and purpose, ability to influence, courage and tenacity are necessary for all leaders whether one is leading a secular organisation or a faith based one. There is, however, something that distinguishes faith based leadership and generic leadership. In addition, Kingdom leadership as taught by Jesus stands out as having unique requirements that differentiate it from the requirements of any other creed. The predecessor of this book, *Learning to Lead for a Better World,* deals with generic leadership or leadership that applies to all categories of people and organisations. Both people learning to lead for secular organisations and disciples of Jesus learning to lead for the Kingdom, would do well to learn and understand the principles set out in that book. However, leadership for the Kingdom presents additional demands over and above those required for generic leadership. We begin with principles that inform leadership for the Kingdom.

# Foundations of Kingdom Leadership Principles

## Some Salient Features of Kingdom Leadership

*The Leadership Role of Kingdom Citizens*

Jesus was sent to set us free from the Kingdom of Satan. All who follow him have been saved by His blood and by His cross. But there is a perpetual cosmic war between the Kingdom of God and the Kingdom of Satan. Now, Jesus wants His followers to join forces with Him in this cosmic war – the war of winning souls for God by leading people to the wonderful light of the Good News, the Gospel of Christ. In this way, Christians have become leaders called to lead others to this wonderful light of Christ. It is important to understand that by virtue of being followers of Jesus, we have been assigned a leadership role in our natural states and in the world. But our leadership role is not that of ruling the world; our role is that of leading people to the Kingdom; of showing the world the way back to the Kingdom we lost when we rebelled against God, and were thrown out of Paradise.

That the citizens of the Kingdom, the followers of Christ, have a leadership role in the world is clear from the following and other scripture passages:

1. "You are the salt of the earth. But if the salt loses its saltiness, how can it become salty again? It is no longer good for anything, except to be thrown out and trampled underfoot.

    "You are the light of the world. A town built on a hill cannot be hidden. Neither do people light a lamp and put it under a bowl. Instead, they put it on its stand, and it gives light to everyone in the house. In the same way, let your light shine before others, that they may

# Learning to lead for the Kingdom

see your good deeds and glorify your Father in heaven"
(Matthew 5:13-16).

This is a passage that was discussed earlier, but it is so
important, there is more that needs to be explained: The
images of salt and light are very significant. Nothing could
express more effectively the impact that the followers of Jesus
are expected to make on the world. Salt permeates the food we
eat and makes it tasty and appetizing. Citizens of the Kingdom
are supposed to have such an effect on the world they live in.
Through their influence, the world should be more livable: the
gospel should be preached and heard; suffering should be
alleviated; those suffering from illness should experience relief;
there should be more justice and less oppression in society.
The image of light denotes we should show the way. By the
way we live, we should shine like a city built on a hill so that
there is no doubt as to what it means to be a Christian
community. A Christian community should be like a lighthouse
that guides all seafarers and warns them of any danger they may
be facing. By the way we behave and conduct ourselves, the
world should be led to see the goodness of God and glorify the
Father. The images of salt and light are so important to the role
of Kingdom citizens in the world, we shall return to them in
the final chapter of the book.

## Spirituality in Kingdom Leadership

From 2006 to 2012, Teboho (my late wife) and I ran a
small leadership academy in Pretoria called the Lead and
Inspire School of Leadership. When the academy was
accredited by the relevant structures of the South African
Government to offer diploma level qualifications in
Leadership, we and our fellow tutors, designed two types of
diplomas, a Diploma in Generic Leadership and a Diploma in
Christian Leadership. In the latter, we found it necessary to

# Foundations of Kingdom Leadership Principles

make a distinction between "Spiritual Christian Leadership" and what we called "General Christian Leadership." We were aware of the possibility of being considered judgmental, but we were also alive to the existence of many professed Christians who hold positions of influence in Christian organisations, and even in the Church, but whose ethics, character and behaviour are no different from those of people who do not believe in Christ. It is not uncommon for Christians in positions of authority to fail to integrate their leadership practices with the essentials of their Christian beliefs. We were indeed also aware of the fact that many non-believers in positions of authority are a lot more exemplary in their morality and actions than many who claim to be followers of Jesus.

We also endeavoured to help our students understand the difference between being "religious" and being "spiritual." Religious practice or "religion" includes such things as attending religious services, participating in ceremonies, prayer meetings of various kinds, singing in the choir etc. One can do all these things and more without being spiritual. One can be devoted to a church or religious organisation without experiencing a personal relationship with God, without experiencing a change of heart, without demonstrating the characteristics of someone who is merciful, who shows love to others, and who is kind and forgiving. Leonard Doohan (2007:37) has correctly said, "Leadership is not simply what we do, but who we are, and what we do because of who we are." This speaks to the character of a spiritual leader. His/her spirituality determines what they do and how they do what they do. It is in this regard that Alan Nelson (2002:52) has put it this way, "Spiritual leaders rely on God, lead to serve, take risks out of faith rather than ego, and listen to the Spirit regarding timing, decisions and relationship issues."

What, then, is spirituality? What we mean by spiritual leadership and a spiritual person is a big subject on which

109

volumes of books are being published. For our purposes here, I shall quote the following: In *Come, Follow Me* (Ngara 2001a:58) I wrote, "Spirituality as conceived of here, refers to a process of developing a deep and personal relationship with God. It entails cultivating a greater consciousness of the nature and qualities of God, experiencing God's presence and striving to be more like God..." We are created in God's image, and part of the purpose of life in the second phase of the kingdom is to strive to grow in spirituality so that we reflect godliness more and more in our own lives, and this entails a fundamental change of heart and mind. According to the Lead and Inspire Facilitator's Manual, "A spiritual person has undergone a transformation, a change in mind, attitude and thought which affects his/her value system and his/her relationship with God and fellow human beings in a fundamental way." (Lead and Inspire 2010:6.)

This discussion leads to an important passage in Scripture which explains what it means to become a spiritual person. In his letter to the Ephesians Paul says, "You were taught, with regard to your former way of life, to put off your old self, which is being corrupted by its deceitful desires; to be made new in the attitude of your minds; and to put on the new self, created to be like God in true righteousness and holiness." (Eph 4:22-24). This is a deep and radical transformation, showing a fundamental departure from the old to the new. This is what it means to be born again (See John 3:3-15). We have reached this point in order to show two things: first, that the demands of Kingdom leadership go much deeper than the demands of generic leadership. Leadership for the Kingdom entails more than the development of qualities and skills, as it demands a total change in who we are to become a new person. Second, Jesus is the supreme example of what it means to be a spiritual person. To lead like Jesus in part entails incorporating both the principles that informed His approach to leadership, and what

# Foundations of Kingdom Leadership Principles

He taught about leadership. In this chapter we focus on the principles that informed His style of leadership. With this understanding, we can then go on to listen to His pronouncements on leadership, which is the focus of the next chapter.

## Some Key Aspects of Jesus' Character and Approach to His Mission

Our intention in the rest of this chapter is to take a brief look at how Jesus saw Himself as a leader with a mission, as a Son of God; and what He saw as His relationship to those He led. In this regard, I will briefly look at seven key aspects of His life and leadership style:

### 1. Jesus and His Mission - Commitment

First, Jesus came with a mission – to bring the news of the Kingdom of God to the world and to lead all who believed Him to the Father. "Yet to all who did receive him, to those who believed in his name, he gave the right to become children of God – children born not of natural descent, nor of human decision or a husband's will, but born of God" (John 1:12). He was sent as a sign and expression of God's love for fallen humankind, "For God so loved the world that he gave his one and only Son, that whoever believes in him shall not perish but have eternal life" (John 3:16).

Jesus knew that the mission He came on was not His own mission, but the Father's mission. On many occasions He explained that His teaching was not His own, but the Father's. For example, when people expressed wonder at the knowledge He had without having been taught, He did not give credit to Himself;

instead, He confessed, "My teaching is not my own. It comes from the One who sent Me" (John 7: 15-16). He also declared, "For I did not speak on my own, but the Father who sent me commanded me to say all that I have spoken" (John 12:49) Before His arrest He told His disciples, "These words you hear are not my own; they belong to the Father who sent me" (John 14:24).

Thus Jesus regarded Himself as a messenger, and a messenger who was wholly and totally committed to the Father's mission. He was so committed to it that it was that which sustained Him in the same way that food sustains our lives. When on one occasion His disciples asked Him to eat, He answered in this manner: "'My food,' said Jesus, is to do the will of him who sent me and to finish his work" (John 4:34). His zeal for the mission can be seen in this statement, "I have come to bring fire on the earth, and how I wish it were already kindled" (Luke 12:49). It was for this mission that He gave up His life and was crucified like a criminal. And so as He hang on the cross just before He breathed His last, He said, "It is finished" (John 19:30). He had completed the mission for which the Father had sent Him into the world.

### 2. Jesus as a Follower

A related issue is that Jesus took every opportunity to be with His Father in prayer. The following are examples: Before He started His public ministry, He fasted for 40 days and 40 nights. Before asking His disciples who they thought He was when Peter declared him to be the Messiah, He had been praying in private (See Luke 9:18). Before the transfiguration He had been praying (See Luke 9:28-29). Immediately before His arrest, He was praying in the Garden of Gethsemani (See Luke 22: 39-46). I have cited Luke's Gospel here, but these events are recorded by the other evangelists as well. The purpose of making this point is to explain that Jesus was not only a leader, but a good follower. His mission was given to Him by the Father, and He made a point of always being in touch with the Father, no doubt to get guidance from the Father. It was by being a good and faithful follower that Jesus became the great leader that He was.

### 3. Jesus and the Holy Spirit

We have just summarized Jesus' loyalty to the Father. He had an equally close relationship with the other person of the Trinity, the Holy Spirit, as He was filled by the Spirit in all He did. First, when He was baptized, "the Holy Spirit descended on him in bodily form like a dove." At that point, a voice came from heaven, "You are my Son, whom I love; with you I am well pleased" (Luke 3:22). It is clear the Trinity was present on this occasion: Father, Son and the Holy Spirit. Thereafter, "Jesus, full of the Holy Spirit, left the Jordan and was led by the Spirit into the wilderness." As He was tempted by the devil, He was led by the Spirit in His responses in terms of which, as already explained, He remained steadfastly loyal to God the Father.

After He had been tempted by the devil and proved His loyalty to the Father, He returned to Galilee "In the power of the Holy Spirit" (Luke 4:14). And when He first announced His mission, He chose a passage which opens with the words, "The Spirit of the Lord is on me" (Luke 4:18). On the night of the

Last Supper, He told His disciples that this same Spirit would continue His (Jesus') work and remind them of everything He had taught them: "But the Advocate, the Holy Spirit, whom the Father will send in my name, will teach you all things and will remind you of everything I have said to you" (John 14:26).

### 4. Humility – His View of Himself as Messiah

The third dimension of His life is that while He was in the very nature of God, consubstantial with the Father, and while all things were created through Him, He chose to come as a humble human being, of the same substance as Adam. He left His heavenly glory to descend to our level, not just as a human being, but as a poor child born in a manger of a poor country girl. There was nothing showy about Him. We have already referred to His temptation by the devil who, among other things, was inviting Jesus to appear to humanity as a showy Saviour who does spectacular things like jumping down from the highest point of the Temple. This would have been in line with the kind of Messiah the Jewish leaders were expecting – a strong, powerful man who would free them from the oppression of the Romans and other nations. Jesus rejected this, and when He went to Jerusalem as King, He did not go there on a mighty steed, but on a humble donkey (See John 12:15). This was to fulfil what had been prophesied by Zechariah: "See, your King comes to you, righteous and victorious, lowly and riding on a donkey, on a colt, the foal of a donkey" (Zechariah 9:9).

The humility of Jesus is recorded in Philippians 2: "In your relationships with one another, have the same mindset as Christ Jesus: Who, being in very nature God, did not consider equality with God something to be used to his own advantage; rather, he made himself nothing by taking the very nature of a servant, being made in human likeness. And being found in appearance as a man, he humbled himself by becoming obedient to death – even death on a cross!" (Philippians 2: 5-8).

This amazing and baffling attitude and behaviour of the Son of God, the Son of God Almighty, he through whom all things were made, is what Henri Nouwen has called *downward mobility*. It is the very opposite of human attitudes and behaviour. We all want to be considered important; we want power; we want to be great; we want glory. We yearn for *upward mobility*. But of Jesus Nouwen (2007:31) says, "He moved from power to powerlessness, from greatness to smallness, from success to failure, from strength to weakness, from glory to ignominy". How different this is from the attitude and behaviour of Satan who rebels against God! The Prophet Isaiah identifies Satan with the King of Babylon in the following passage:

'How you have fallen from heaven, morning star, Son of the dawn! You have been cast down to the earth, You who once laid low the nations! You said in your heart, "I will ascend to the heavens; I will raise my throne above the stars of God; I will sit enthroned on the mount of assembly, on the utmost heights of Mount Zaphon. I will ascend above the tops of the clouds; I will make myself like the Most High."' (Isa 14:12-14).

# Learning to lead for the Kingdom

### 5.  *Courage in Defence of the Truth*

The expression "the courage of your convictions" is exemplified in Jesus. He was a man of courage who demonstrated His courage in every situation where the truth needed to be expressed: whether He was talking to the Pharisees (See Mark 7:1-13); or to the generality of Jewish leaders and crowds (See John 6:25-59); or to His own disciples (See John 6:60-70). There was no compromise with the truth even if it meant people were to desert Him as in the case of His disciples just quoted. The truth had to be confirmed and defended even before the High Priest and authorities like Pontius Pilate (John 18: 19-37; 19:11).

### 6.  *An Exemplary Leader who Walked his Talk*

In a previous publication (Ngara 2004: 56-58) I explained that Jesus had a striking character, but that it was not just the force of character that attracted people to Him. What was even more important, was that He was an exemplary leader who walked His talk. There were no contradictions in Him. His teaching and His actions were consistent with one another. The Marxist writer, Milan Machovec, eloquently explained that Jesus convinced His disciples to be loyal to Him because He was a role model who was the very embodiment of the values of the Kingdom of God that He preached.

# Foundations of Kingdom Leadership Principles

### 7. *Jesus the Supreme Example of Servant Leadership*

As far as we know, Jesus was the originator of the principles and practice of servant leadership. He was the first to articulate and demonstrate the principles of this form of leadership. We shall elaborate on these principles in the next chapter. At this juncture, it will suffice to make the following points: Jesus' life was characterised by a spirit of service. He suffered and died for the sake of humankind. As we shall see, He officially and solemnly instituted servant leadership as the form of leadership that His followers should practise when He washed His disciples' feet and said, "I have set you an example that you should do as I have done for you" (John 13:15). Of Himself He said, "For even the Son of Man did not come to be served, but to serve, and to give His life as a ransom for many" (Mark 10:45). We shall discuss the significance of these statements in the next chapter.

## Implications for Kingdom Leadership

The point of explaining the principles outlined in this chapter is to suggest that if we are to play our role as authentic leaders for the Kingdom, we cannot lead in a way that is different from Jesus' way. We must pay attention to the following:

1. First, Jesus' mission was given to Him by the Father; it was not His own mission. Similarly, we cannot come up with our own missions. Each one of us must discover the mission given to her/him by the Lord and know that it is not their own personal mission. We must each one of us fulfil our mission as the Lord

117

wants us to. As noted in *Learning to Lead for a Better World,* "Each one of us has been given a life and it demands we fulfil the purpose for which it was given to us" (Ngara, 2019:97-98). As pointed out in the same book, Victor Frankl reminds us that life is a concrete assignment which demands fulfilment (p.97). Leadership for the Kingdom is certainly an assignment, and as we seek to fulfil that assignment, we must be guided by Jesus' sense of commitment which led Him to declare, "My food ... is to do the will of him who sent me and to finish his work" (John 4:34).

2. Second, to be a leader of the Kingdom, one must first learn to be a follower. Jesus was a loyal follower of the Father. The first thing we must learn to do before we seek to lead others to the Kingdom, is to be a true disciple of Jesus – to follow the Master. We cannot do otherwise because Jesus says to us, "Very truly, I tell you, no servant is greater than his master, nor is a messenger greater than the one who sent him" (John 13:16). In fact, Jesus expects us to be replicas of Himself. As Henri Nouwen puts it, "Indeed to live a spiritual life means to become living Christs. It is not enough to imitate Christ as much as possible... No, the spiritual life presents us with a far more radical demand: to be living Christs here and now, in time and history" (Nouwen 2007:20).

3. Third, just as Jesus was guided by the Holy Spirit, we can do nothing without the guidance of the Holy Spirit. Knowledge of the Kingdom does not depend on our natural intelligence; we have no wisdom of our own in spiritual matters. It is the Spirit of Christ that

118

enlightens us, empowers us and gives us wisdom to lead as the followers of Christ and citizens of the Kingdom should: "In the same way no one knows the thoughts of God except the Spirit of God. We have not received the spirit of the world but the Spirit who is from God, that we may understand what God has freely given us" (1 Corinthians 2:11-12).

4.  Fourth, to fulfil His mission, Jesus followed the downward mobility principle- humility - the way of the cross. In this regard, we shall see that His teaching on leadership is completely in line with the downward mobility principle. In the world, the drive for upward mobility is taken as the norm: we want to be popular, to be competitive, to be famous, to be spectacular, to be regarded as bosses etc. As we shall see, leadership for the Kingdom demands that we adopt the opposite of such attitudes and behaviours.

5.  Fifth, leading people to the Kingdom in our time, demands of one to be a courageous person. Jesus preached the Kingdom in a hostile environment. What He taught was contrary to the values of both the Romans and the Jewish leaders of the time. It is reasonable to argue that as a pagan people, the Romans would not have been as worried about Jesus' teaching; what could have been a concern was if the teaching was a threat to the Roman political establishment – which is why the Jewish leaders were accusing Him of opposing Caesar (See John 19: 12).The truth, however, was that Jesus' teaching was a threat to the religious (and political) authority of the Jewish leaders. Teaching about the Kingdom of God in its true sense in our time flies in the face of the

values of most people in our societies and can be a threat to political leaders. Furthermore, there are societies today which are openly opposed to the Gospel message of Jesus – this may be on religious grounds as in Moslem countries, or on ideological grounds, as in Marxist oriented states, such as China. In all these situations, one needs to have the kind of courage that Jesus had, if one is to teach and uphold the values of the Kingdom.

6. Sixth, courage is buttressed by character. It is a person of character who becomes a role model, because character gives one principles that guide one's behaviour. "Character is built on the principles of integrity, accountability, honesty and respectability" (Ngara 2019:42). Integrity means doing the right thing no matter what. We have already referred to Jesus' integrity in explaining that He stood by the truth no matter who He was talking to –whether to the Pharisees, the generality of the Jews, Roman officials or even to His own disciples. By behaving in this way, He also demonstrated what an honest person He was. His honesty and accountability were also evident in the way He always declared that His teaching was not His own but came from the Father.

7. Finally, those who regard themselves as leaders in our world behave as bosses of the people they lead. They like to be respected and worshipped, and to take the highest places at functions, dinners and meetings. Jesus came with a very different approach to leadership – He came as a servant who serves, and He expects citizens of the kingdom to follow His example.

## Foundations of Kingdom Leadership Principles

As we listen to what Jesus says about leadership for the kingdom, we should hear Him saying to us, "Walk in my footsteps. This is what I am and what I do as a leader; do likewise; be a replica of me."

# Learning to lead for the Kingdom

# CHAPTER FIVE

# Jesus' Teaching on Leadership for the Kingdom

## *Two Categories of Leaders in Jesus' Teaching*

In talking about Jesus' teaching on leadership, it helps to make a distinction between the leadership role of all His followers and the approach to leadership by people who hold positions of leadership in society and in the church. The distinction is not a very neat one because, as already indicated, there is a level at which every follower of Jesus, every citizen of the Kingdom, is called upon to play a leadership role wherever he/she is. There are also categories of people in society who do not necessarily hold positions of influence, but are important for the existence and development of human society. For example, parents and teachers have important leadership roles to play in society and what we say about leadership applies as much to these two categories of people, as it does to people who hold such positions of influence as pastors, heads of schools, business leaders, heads of denominations etc.

In talking about leadership, Jesus was clearly aware of the leadership roles of what He called His disciples – all His

# Learning to lead for the Kingdom

followers, not just the twelve, on the one hand; and on the other, what society regarded as "leaders", i.e. people who held positions of authority and influence such as the Pharisees, the Teachers of the Law, the High Priest, the Roman governors etc. When He gave the command "You are the salt of the earth... You are the light of the world..." He was addressing not only His disciples, but also "the crowds" who had gathered there (See Matthew 5:1-2). In some of the passages, we are going to discuss, Jesus was clearly referring to the people who held positions of authority, and this was partly because some of the twelve, if not all of them, saw themselves holding important positions in what they thought was the kind of Kingdom He was going to establish.

It is instructive that in training His disciples to preach the good news, Jesus made a distinction between the twelve, the apostles, who were going to be the leaders of His Church, and the seventy-two others, who represent the generality of His disciples. He first sent out the twelve, and "Gave them power and authority to drive out all demons and to cure diseases, and he sent them out to proclaim the Kingdom of God and to heal the sick ..."(Luke 9: 1-11). Later on, He "Appointed seventy-two others and sent them two by two ahead of him to every town and place where he was about to go" (Luke 10: 1-24). It is to these seventy-two that He said, "The harvest is plentiful, but the workers are few. Ask the Lord of the harvest, therefore, to send out workers into his harvest field" (Luke 10:2).

One thing that is clear in these two Scripture passages, is that bringing the Kingdom of God to people in the transitional phase, includes both proclaiming the good news on the one hand, and on the other, casting out demons, curing diseases

# Jesus' Teaching on Leadership for the Kingdom

and healing the sick. This further clarifies the fact that illnesses, blindness, being possessed by demons etc, are associated with the work of Satan. Consequently, casting out demons is defeating the work of the devil. Hence, when the seventy-two report, "Lord, even the demons submit to us in your name", His response is, "I saw Satan fall like lightning from heaven. I have given you authority to trample on snakes and scorpions and to overcome all the power of the enemy; nothing will harm you..." (Luke 10:17-20). These powers are given, not only to those who hold positions of authority in the Church, but may also be granted by the Lord to some members of the group I have referred to above, as "the generality of His disciples", such as the seventy-two were.

It is interesting that after Jesus had expressed His joy to the Father for revealing these things to "little children", He then turned to His disciples, namely, the twelve, and said to them *"privately"*, "Blessed are the eyes that see what you see ..." (Luke 10:23-24). The apostles were therefore, a special group of leaders, and it is to this group that He articulated the leadership principles that we are going to discuss in the rest of this chapter. The point must be made, though, that while the principles were articulated to those who were to be the leaders of His Church, they apply to all categories of Jesus' disciples – to all citizens of the Kingdom.

## Jesus' Pronouncements on Leadership

In discussing Jesus' teaching on leadership, we shall focus on the following: Mark 10:35-45; Luke 22:24-27; John 13:1-17; and John 15:12-15. Reference may also be made to other passages, such as Matthew 20:20-28 and Mark 9:33-37.

# Learning to lead for the Kingdom

*The Request of the Sons of Zebedee*

'Then James and John, the sons of Zebedee, came to Him. "Teacher," they said to him, "we want you to do for us whatever we ask." "What do you want me to do for you?" he asked. They replied, "Let one of us sit at your right hand and the other at your left in your glory."

"You don't know what you are asking," Jesus said. "Can you drink the cup I drink or be baptized with the baptism I am baptized with?" "We can," they answered. Jesus said to them, "You will drink the cup I drink and be baptized with the baptism I am baptized with, but to sit at my right or left is not for me to grant. These places belong to those for whom they have been prepared." When the ten heard about this, they became indignant with James and John. Jesus called them together and said, "You know that those who are regarded as rulers of the Gentiles lord it over them, and their high officials exercise authority over them. Not so with you. Instead, whoever wants to become great among you must be your servant, and whoever wants to be first must be slave of all. For even the Son of Man did not come to be served, but to serve, and to give his life as a ransom for many." (Mark 10:35-45).

The context of this passage is very important. The idea of leadership that the sons of Zebedee had was the same as that of the Gentiles: Among the Gentiles then, and among the rest of humanity now, important people occupy important positions and exercise authority over those under them. Similarly, James and John were thinking of occupying important positions when Jesus was in power, and being the second in command, as it were. In Matthew's account, the mother of the two disciples was involved. She even knelt down

# Jesus' Teaching on Leadership for the Kingdom

to make the request for her sons (See Matthew 20:20-23). Much as they had been with Jesus for a long time, their view of leadership was still the normal "worldly" view of leadership. The other ten, were evidently of the same view, and were indignant with James and John for asking Jesus to favour them by giving them the second highest positions in the Kingdom that was coming.

It must have been a surprise and disappointment for all of them when Jesus introduced the concept of servant leadership: "Instead, whoever wants to become great among you must be your servant, and whoever wants to be first must be slave of all." This must have been a very new concept of leadership – to associate greatness with servanthood and top position with slavery! And it must also have been bewildering, or perhaps confusing, to hear their Lord and Master saying He came to serve, not to be served and even to give His life "as a ransom." The concept of servant leadership has become widely known in the modern world, but I am not aware of any thinker, philosopher or leader who talked about it before Jesus. And while the concept in both its secular and religious sense, is now well known, particularly after the publication of Robert Greenleaf's book (Greenleaf 1977), Jesus' explanation and practice of it was much more radical than our concept of it.

*The Disciples Argue about Who among them should be Considered the Greatest*

'A dispute also arose among them as to which of them was considered to be the greatest.

127

# Learning to lead for the Kingdom

Jesus said to them, "The kings of the Gentiles lord it over them; and those who exercise authority over them call themselves Benefactors. But you are not to be like that. Instead, the greatest among you should be like the youngest, and the one who rules like the one who serves. For who is greater, the one who is at the table or the one who serves? Is it not the one at the table? But I am among you as the one who serves. You are those who have stood by me in my trials. And I confer on you a kingdom, just as my Father conferred one on me, so that you may eat and drink at my table in my kingdom and sit on thrones, judging the twelve tribes of Israel'" (Luke 22:24-30).

This passage reveals a number of important issues: First, like James and John, all the Apostles at this stage had a very secular view of leadership. Like James and John in the previous passage, they were looking forward to a Kingdom that Jesus would establish on earth in their life time, and they saw themselves having important positions in that Kingdom. Furthermore, they were in competition with one another for greatness, with perhaps some of them or each one of them thinking they were greater than the rest of the team. What this also reveals is that at this stage their loyalty to Jesus was probably not entirely selfless. Each expected a reward for his loyalty.

Second, as in the previous passage, here Jesus presents a stark contrast between the conception of leadership in the world and what should be the view of leadership among His followers in the second phase of the Kingdom of God. Citizens of the Kingdom who hold positions of authority and influence in this world, should regard themselves not as those who are served, but as the ones who serve. According to this view of leadership, the guest who goes to have a sumptuous dinner in a restaurant should regard himself or herself as less important than the waiter who takes the order of the guest and brings the meal to the table for the guest to enjoy. In a family, the oldest member should behave as though they are the youngest. In terms of this logic, the president of a country should serve the lowest members of society such as workers and peasants; and the CEO of a company should serve the lower level workers such as labourers, gardeners, cleaners and cooks. Jesus was the master of the disciples, but gave Himself the position of their servant.

The explanation just given points to an important principle of Jesus that we have already discussed – the downward mobility principle and the virtue of humility. This does not apply to leadership only; it applies to every aspect of life, including behaviour at social gatherings such as meals: Consequently, "When someone invites you to a wedding feast, do not take the place of honour, for a person more distinguished than you may have been invited. If so, the host who invited both of you will come and say to you, 'Give this person your seat.' Then, humiliated, you will have to take the least important place. But when you are invited, take the lowest place, so that when your host comes, he will say to you, 'Friend, move up to a better place.' Then you will be honoured in the presence of all the other guests. *For all those who exalt themselves will be humbled, and those who humble themselves will be exalted.*" (Luke 14:7-11; *italics used for emphasis*). But the principle applies, not only to guests, but to hosts as well. So when you give a banquet "invite the poor, the crippled, the lame, the blind, and you will be blessed" (Luke 14:12-14).

# Learning to lead for the Kingdom

Going back to the principal passage under discussion (See Luke 22:24-27), we should notice that there is a further development: Those who put themselves in the place of servants in this life, will find themselves as leaders in the final and eternal Kingdom of God. He, Jesus, who was in very nature God, made Himself nothing by taking the very nature of a servant, by becoming human, and humbled Himself further by becoming obedient to the extent of dying the most disreputable death – death on a cross! Because of this, God exalted him to the highest place (See Philippians 2:6-11). At the renewal of all things, this same Son of Man, who came to earth as a slave, will be a King and "will sit on his glorious throne" (Matthew 25:31) having had the Kingdom conferred upon Him by the Father. Similarly, if the Apostles were to regard themselves as servants in this second phase of the Kingdom, they will have the Kingdom conferred upon them by the Son of Man, and they will sit at His table and drink and eat at His table, and will sit on thrones, *judging the twelve tribes of Israel*. Thus, those who regard themselves as Kings in this world will be judged by these former fishermen.

## *Jesus Institutes Servant Leadership*

'It was just before the Passover Festival. Jesus knew that the hour had come for him to leave this world and go to the Father. Having loved His own who were in the world, he loved them to the end. The evening meal was in progress, and the devil had already prompted Judas, the son of Simon Iscariot, to betray Jesus. Jesus knew that the Father had put all things under his power, and that he had come from God and was returning to God; so he got up from the meal, took off his outer clothing, and wrapped a towel around his waist. After that he poured water into a basin and began to wash his disciples' feet, drying them with the towel that was wrapped around him.

He came to Simon Peter who said to him, "Lord, are you going to wash my feet?" Jesus replied, "You do not realize now what I am doing, but later you will understand." "No," said Peter, "you shall never wash my feet." Jesus said, "Unless I wash you, you have no part with me." "Then, Lord," Simon Peter replied, "not just my feet but my hands and my head as well!" Jesus answered, "Those who have had a bath need only to wash their feet; their whole body is clean. And you are clean, though not every one of you." For he knew who was going to betray him, and that was why he said not everyone was clean.

When he had finished washing their feet, he put on his clothes and returned to his place. "Do you understand what I have done for you?" he asked them. "You call me 'Teacher' and 'Lord,' and rightly so, for that is what I am. Now that I, your Lord and Teacher, have washed your feet, you also should wash one another's feet. I have set you an example that you should do as I have done for you. Very truly I tell you, no servant is greater than his master, nor is a messenger greater than the one who sent him. Now that you know these things, you will be blessed if you do them.'" (John 13:1-17).

This is a very key passage in a number of respects: First, unlike in the first two key passages we have discussed, here Jesus does not only teach about servant leadership; He demonstrates in actual practice what it means to be a servant leader. In the first two passages, He teaches by word; in this passage, He teaches by both word and deed. Matthew quotes

# Learning to lead for the Kingdom

Him as saying, "Whoever does not take up their cross and follow me is not worthy of me," and all four gospels relate how he carried His cross to the place of His crucifixion. In the passage from Luke discussed above He says, "I am among you as one who serves." If the disciples did not understand what He meant then, they should have now, in terms of John's account, fully understood Him when He rose from the table, put a towel around His waist and began to wash their feet.

The second point is related to the first: In this and other passages, Jesus shows that He is an exemplary leader who leads from the front. There is nothing that He expects His disciples to do which He does not Himself do. In this example, the roles are changed: The disciples were His followers; they called Him "Lord" and "Teacher", but here, He was kneeling down before them and washing their dirty feet! In this regard, as impulsive as He was, Peter was quite right to say, "Lord, are you going to wash my feet?"; adding, "No, you shall never wash my feet." Mind you, Jesus had earlier confirmed as correct Peter's insightful and Spirit filled designation of Him as "the Messiah, the Son of the living God" (Matthew 16:16-20). It was therefore unthinkable, that this person whom the disciples regarded as their future King could stoop to do the work of a slave! When He then said, "Now that I, your Lord and Teacher, have washed your feet, you also should wash one another's feet", there was no way they could say this was too low a job to do. He was the Master and they were servants who could not be greater than their Master. He had indeed "set an example" for them to do what He had done for them.

The third point we shall discuss, is that the passage has correctly been taken by the Christian Church as an important

# Jesus' Teaching on Leadership for the Kingdom

passage in that washing feet has become part of the tradition of the Church. In some churches the feet washing ceremony is conducted on Maundy Thursday, the Thursday before Good Friday. The normal practice is that, as part of the Maundy Thursday ceremony, the priest / pastor washes the feet of twelve people who may be volunteers or may have been previously selected for the purpose. Normally, once the twelve people have had their feet washed, they go back to their places in the church and the rest of the ceremony continues.

The practice is a very good one, but I am of the strong view that the Church does not go far enough in marking the importance of this ceremony. In some churches the occasion of the Last Supper as recorded in the Gospels of Matthew (Matthew 26:26-29); Mark (Mark 14:22-25); and Luke (Luke 22:14-20) is taken as the occasion when Jesus instituted the Sacrament of the Eucharist (Holy Communion) and the Sacrament of Holy Orders (the Priesthood). John does not record this event, but is the only evangelist who gives a detailed account of Jesus' washing of the disciples' feet. The account is just as dignified and sombre as the accounts on the Last Supper and is even more detailed. No doubt, John could remember this as one of the most important events in Jesus' life with His disciples. However, the Church takes the washing of feet as a mere ritual which is not accorded the same importance as the Last Supper. I am convinced the Spirit has led me to believe that the washing of feet was not only an act by which Jesus demonstrated the importance of washing each other's feet. On the contrary, *by this act Jesus formerly instituted the practice of servant leadership.*

# Learning to lead for the Kingdom

Jesus was not only addressing the twelve, but all His disciples for all time when He said, "I have set you an example that you should do as I have done for you," and "Now that you know these things, you will be blessed if you do them." Gene Wilkes (1998:9) has correctly commented, "The essential lesson I learned from Jesus on leadership was that *he taught and embodied leadership as service."* In the passage under discussion, Jesus is teaching His followers to embody service in every situation. We should serve our countries, our organisations, our communities, our churches and our families; and we should serve one another. The washing of feet on Maundy Thursday and on any other day, should give us an opportunity to reflect on the extent to which we have fulfilled Jesus' command in our lives and on what we are going to do in order to act and conduct ourselves as servants in the various situations in which we find ourselves. We should be towel leaders, holding our towels like Jesus to serve all who come into our sphere of influence. As we perform our social obligations as briefly summarized in Chapter 3, we should do so in a spirit of service. Those of us in positions of authority should perform their duties in a spirit of service to the people they lead.

The characteristics of a servant leader in the generic sense as outlined in the predecessor of this book (Ngara 2019:85-87), apply equally to the followers of Christ, except that there is a greater demand on those who call themselves disciples of Jesus or citizens of the Kingdom. For them, servant leadership also entails carrying their cross and understanding that greatness lies in reducing oneself to the level of a humble towel leader following in the footsteps of the Master who stoops to wash the dirty feet of His own subordinates. As "the salt of the earth" and "the light of the world", the followers of Jesus should help to raise the flag of servant leadership, set new standards for it and influence the world to see it as the highest form of leadership that should be promoted in our educational institutions, churches and work places.

### *The Command to Love and Bear Fruit*

"My command is this: Love each other as I have loved you. Greater love has no one than this: to lay down one's life for one's friends. You are my friends if you do what I command. I no longer call you servants, because a servant does not know his master's business. Instead, I have called you friends, for everything that I learned from my Father I have made known to you. You did not choose me, but I chose you and appointed you so that you might go and bear fruit – fruit that will last – and so that whatever you ask in my name the Father will give you. This is my command: love each other" (John 15:12-17).

In this passage, Jesus was not addressing the subject of leadership as in the other three, but He was talking to His disciples as leaders of the Kingdom. By this time, Judas had already left to go and bring those who were going to arrest Jesus, and so the Lord was addressing the eleven. He talked to them about many things as recorded in chapters 14 to 16 of John's Gospel: For example, He explained that He is the way to the Father; He promised the Holy Spirit; He explained the important principle of the vine and its branches; He warned the disciples that the world would hate them; and about how their sorrow would turn to joy. Why, then, focus on John 15:12-17?

# Learning to lead for the Kingdom

The passage brings in some dimensions that are not covered by the first three: First, the commandment to love. Kingdom leaders must learn to love, not only other people, but one another. As a team, they should be seen as a team of leaders who love one another to the extent of being prepared to lay down their lives for one another just as He was going to lay down His own life for them. Second, Jesus was not the kind of Master who wants to be feared by His followers, who treats His disciples as servants. In the leadership of domination, as explained in the predecessor to this book (Ngara 2019:63), the leader exercises control of subordinates by using subtle or overt threats; to keep power, the leader instils fear in other people. As pointed out in the same book (Ibid: 61), one of Machiavelli's dictums was "If you have to make a choice, to be feared is much safer than to be loved." As the supreme servant leader, Jesus tells His disciples, "I no longer call you servants … Instead, I have called you friends." Citizens of the Kingdom do not have to treat Jesus as a haughty leader who wants to be worshipped by frightened followers as some leaders in our time do. As Kingdom citizens, we can be relaxed with Jesus and treat Him as a brother and a friend. But as friends, we should feel the urge to reciprocate; we should return His friendship with a commitment to obey His command. He clearly says to us, "You are my friends if you do what I command", and we should take that requirement seriously.

The third point is extremely important: The Apostles were not the ones who chose Jesus – He chose them, and He chose and appointed them so that they might go and bear fruit that endures. In this regard, those of us in positions of authority must be conscious of the fact that it is Jesus who chooses us, and He chooses us so that we may go and bear fruit for the

Kingdom. There is no point in being a leader if you do not advance the cause of the Kingdom. Some are given positions, be it in the Church or in secular society, and all they do is to manage the organisation or institution concerned. At best, the organisation or institution concerned does not deteriorate; in some cases, the entity even deteriorates. There is no attempt or capacity to help the entity to grow qualitatively and quantitatively. In other words, the "leader" does not bear fruit. As Kingdom leaders, Jesus expects us to bear fruit, both as individuals and collectively.

### *Conclusion: Key Points to Remember*

As a conclusion to this chapter, we need to reflect on three key issues that have come up in the chapter:

#### *1.    God and the Downward Mobility*

In the first three passages highlighted in this chapter, we see that Jesus came with a completely new view of leadership. He turned the values of this world upside down by introducing the principles and practice of servant leadership. This should also make us see that for the sake of re-establishing His Kingdom on earth and saving humanity from damnation and the clutches of Satan, God did the completely unexpected and unthinkable: His one and only Son descended from heaven to become human, to be born of a woman, to be born in a cave among animals, and to die the most disreputable death of all – death on a cross! The Son of the Almighty God, the Creator of all things, came among us to die as a slave.

# Learning to lead for the Kingdom

The world thinks in terms of upward mobility, showing power in the manner in which the devil wanted Jesus to fly down from the highest point of the Temple so as to be seen and admired by all as a powerful One . The world thinks in terms of being important and showing off power and being admired and praised. The kind of Messiah the leaders of the Jews wanted to see was one who would do spectacular things. In the mind of humankind, the Jesus who rode into Jerusalem would have been One who came riding on an impressive steed. Instead, Jesus went into Jerusalem riding on a humble colt of a donkey. The Son of Almighty God reduced Himself to a humble and despicable leader. A key aspect of servant leadership is for the leader to reduce himself/herself to the level of a humble servant – a leader without a title.

## 2. *Giving Servant Leadership its Proper Place in the Christian Calendar*

Jesus did not just teach and practice servant leadership – He formerly instituted servant leadership. The Church does well to commemorate the washing of feet on Maundy Thursday. But this does not go far enough. There is a need to commemorate the event in a more significant way. I would suggest that in addition to the Maundy Thursday commemoration, there should be a day dedicated to servant leadership in the church calendar. That day should not just be a celebration or commemoration, but a day on which the followers of Jesus both commemorate the institution of servant leadership and commit themselves in practical terms to the spirit, values and practice of servant leadership.

# Jesus' Teaching on Leadership for the Kingdom

### *The Command to Bear Fruit*

As Kingdom leaders, Jesus expects us to bear fruit, both as individuals and collectively. As a collective, we have a duty to ask ourselves: To what extent have we fulfilled all that Jesus has commanded us to do? It is necessary to sometimes reflect on our performance for the Kingdom by asking the following questions, among others?

- How effectively have we conveyed to the world Jesus' message about the Kingdom of God?
- How effectively have we, the followers of Jesus, played the role of being salt and light to the world? (See Matthew 5:13-16).
- To what extent have we succeeded in making disciples of all nations? (See Matthew 28: 16-20).
- To what extent have we been witnesses of Jesus in Jerusalem, in all Judea and Samaria, and to the ends of the earth? (See Acts 1:7-8).
- How successfully have we gone about feeding the hungry, giving something to drink to the thirsty, inviting strangers in, clothing the naked, looking after the sick and visiting prisoners? (See Matthew 25:31-46).
- Many of the problems of the world in which we live, are due to a serious leadership deficit. To what extent are we promoting servant leadership as the form of leadership that ensures leaders work to serve the interests of the people they represent?
- Jesus prayed passionately that all believers may be one, clarifying that the world will know that the Father sent Him if His followers are brought to complete unity

# Learning to lead for the Kingdom

(See John 17:20-23). How seriously are we working to heal the wounds of our hopeless divisions?

# Jesus' Teaching on Leadership for the Kingdom

# PART II:

# THE COLLECTIVE AND INDIVIDUAL CALL TO SERVE THE KINGDOM

# CHAPTER SIX

※

## Understanding one's Purpose and God's Call

*Humans Are Called for a Purpose*

Many authorities believe that every one of us was created for a purpose. In terms of this, human life has a purpose beyond our daily routines. Human life has a *why*, a reason for existence, and this is what distinguishes humans from other earthly creatures. But it could also be argued that every creature – whether a human being or an animal, bird or fish, everything that moves on the ground and in the water – has a reason for existence: to give glory to God. For God created everything in the beginning for a purpose and saw that it was good. But humankind was created for a very special purpose. Human beings were made in the image of God to rule over all other creatures (See Genesis 1:26-28).

It could be argued, "Yes, God created human beings to rule over other created things, but does this necessarily mean every human being was created for a specific purpose? To this Viktor E. Frankl (1985:131) would answer: "Everyone has his own vocation or mission in life to carry out a concrete assignment which demands fulfilment." In terms of this reference, every individual, great or small, believer or unbeliever, has a purpose in life. The question then might be: Granted that everyone has their own vocation, but does this necessarily mean everyone was *created for* a purpose or was *assigned* a purpose *at birth* or *at conception*? The question whether one was *created for* a purpose or *assigned* one at birth, conception or at any other stage in one's life is neither here nor there. The point is that everyone has a purpose, *a special purpose* over and above the general purpose of humanity having been called to give glory to God by looking after planet earth and ruling over other created living things on the Creator's behalf.

Human life becomes meaningful only in the context of a purpose which one strives to fulfil. This purpose, gives one a sense of responsibility. Viktor Frankl (ibid) would further argue that a human being should not ask what the meaning of life is; rather, it is life that questions everyone what meaning they are giving to life; and the answer to that question lies in *being responsible.* Each person must therefore, ask themselves "for what, to what, or to whom he understands himself to be responsible" (Frankl 1985: 131-132). In simple terms, what is the purpose of my life? Assuming that I get what I think I need in life such as a good job, a fantastic salary, a nice house in an upmarket suburb, and a beautiful or handsome spouse, will this make me feel I have fulfilled the requirements of a happy and meaningful life? If I even go further to raise a family and to meet the requirements of my company and government, will I have fulfilled the requirements of Viktor Frankl's question just quoted above?

# Understanding one's Purpose and God's Call

If Frankl's question applies to every person, it must apply even more so to everyone who holds a position of authority. In particular, every leader must ask themselves: What am I responsible for and to whom am I responsible? Those who understand the concept of God's Kingdom that is discussed in Part I of this book, should ask themselves: What does the life of Jesus and His concept of the Kingdom of God mean to me? What is the significance of my life to God's Kingdom? Am I called to play a role in the task of proclaiming the Kingdom? If I believe I am called to play a role in this regard, what is it that I think I can do in advancing the cause of the Kingdom of God? This requires an understanding of how God calls leaders for the Kingdom.

### How God Calls Leaders

In the case of leadership for the Kingdom, and on the understanding that it is to God that we are responsible, a series of other questions arise, including the following:

- At what point and in what circumstances does God call us for leadership?
- How does God train us?
- Does God equip us for leadership?
- And how does God ensure that we are fit for Kingdom leadership?

There are several principles we should consider in our effort to understand how God calls us. At this stage, we will focus on the following:

### The First Principle: God Calls us Before we are Born

# Learning to lead for the Kingdom

The evidence from the Scriptures points to the fact that God chooses us before we are born. Many of us do not know what is going to finally happen to us and where our leadership responsibilities are going to take us; but God knows. For some people, the call in terms of the vocation they are to follow is clear. They are called to follow a certain vocation such as religious life or teaching, and that is it. For many others, God's call entails following a road that is full of twists and turns. And so, some have a single and straightforward vocation, while others may experience multiple vocations: you are called to one kind of life or profession, you follow it; and then you are called to something else, and then to something else, and so on. In many cases, when God is calling us to do these things, He is preparing us for something that we may not be aware of until much later in life. God is training us through the experiences we are going through.

There is a distinction that we need to make between a vocation and a personal mission. A vocation can be referred to as a profession or a career. One is called to a vocation such as teaching, religious life or political life with many others. Then within that vocation, one feels called to do something special – one feels called to do something specific or unique, which may be referred to as a calling within a calling. That is one's special mission. Mother Teresa, for example, was called to religious life and joined the Loreto Sisters, but eventually she felt strongly drawn to serve the poorest of the poor in India, and she consequently, left the Loreto Sisters to form her own congregation – the Missionary Sisters of Charity. Martin Luther was an Augustinian monk, but eventually he felt a strong urge to study the Bible on certain aspects of salvation, leading him to question some of the practices of the Church of

146

the time, and that eventually led to his becoming a leader of the Reformation. We make this clarification to point to the fact that one's purpose in life is closely related to one's personal mission, and the personal mission is usually related to one's vocation. By this we are not excluding the possibility of special cases when someone is called to pursue something completely outside their vocation.

Whatever the case, God knows our future before we know it. What the Lord said to Prophet Jeremiah, He is saying to all of us that He has called us to be Kingdom leaders: "Before I formed you in the womb I knew you, before you were born I set you apart; I appointed you as a prophet to the nations" (Jeremiah 1:5).

In the Letter to the Ephesians, the Apostle Paul tells us that the Apostles and other leaders were predestined in accordance with God's plan, for He works everything in conformity with the purpose of His will. We are chosen so that God may be glorified (Ephesians 1:4-6; 11-14). In the Letter to the Romans, Paul explains even more clearly that those of us who were called by Him, were called before we were born and that He predestined us to be conformed to the image of His Son: "And we know that in all things God works for the good of those who love him, who have been called according to his purpose. For those God foreknew he also predestined to be conformed to the image of his Son, that he might be the firstborn among many brothers and sisters. And those he predestined he also called; those he called he also justified; those he justified he also glorified" (Romans 8:28-30).

# Learning to lead for the Kingdom

## *The Second Principle: God Uses the Circumstances of our Lives to Train Us*

John Wesley is quoted as having said, "It is not by chance that a man is born at such a time, of such parents and in such a place and condition" (Wakefield 1990:9). The time and birth of a leader are not a coincidence, but are part of God's plan. Let us begin with the life of Jesus Himself: Luke says He decided to write "an orderly account" of the birth and life of Jesus (See Luke 1:3), and it is indeed an orderly account, showing, among other things: The relationship to the birth and work of John the Baptist; the decree issued by Augustus Caesar for a census to be taken; the fact that Joseph was of the house of David, and Bethlehem, the city of David (See Luke 2:1 ff); the genealogy of Jesus back to Adam, "the Son of God" (See Luke 3:21-38). Thus in his account, Luke does not only show the connection between Jesus and what was prophesied about Him (e.g Luke 4:17-21); He also attempts to show the connection between Jesus and "the first Adam" of Paul's teaching (1 Corinthians 15:21-22).

There is more about the time of Jesus' birth and life: The Jews were back from exile and were able to go to Jerusalem for the Festival of Tabernacles, and the Jewish leaders had Him killed in Jerusalem, the Holy City. Significantly too, this was the time when the Roman Empire was at its peak, and this facilitated the spread of the gospel message of Jesus. Furthermore, the Romans had the most cruel and most humiliating method of punishing criminals – crucifixion. By subjecting Himself to death on the cross, Jesus demonstrated the principle of downward mobility in the clearest way possible. And what then happened is that the cross became the

# Understanding one's Purpose and God's Call

most appropriate symbol of the Church He established. This symbol of suffering and humiliation, became the sign by which those who believe in the Kingdom were to be identified.

Consider Jesus' first disciples: Simon Peter and his brother Andrew; and the other brothers, James and John, were all fishermen, and that is how Jesus called them and trained them to be fishers of human beings (See Mark 1: 14-20). And consider the Apostle Paul: Born as some kind of contemporary of Jesus, and as someone who could claim, "I was advancing in Judaism beyond many Jews of my own age, and was extremely zealous for the traditions of my fathers" (Galatians 1:14). It was this man that Jesus appointed the Apostle of the Gentiles. As a learned Roman citizen at this time of the expansion of the Roman Empire, he was able to spread the news of the Kingdom far and wide. He could argue and debate with both Jewish leaders and learned Greeks. As pointed out in an earlier publication (Ngara 2004:60), "In fact, without Paul it is inconceivable as to whether Christianity could have spread to the then known world as rapidly as it did, and whether Christian theology could even be what it is today." We could think of other Kingdom leaders, such as Augustine of Hippo, Martin Luther, Ignatius Loyola, Billy Graham, Mother Teresa and so on. As evidence of the truth of John Wesley's statement quoted above, all these and others lived and worked at a particular point during the second phase of the Kingdom. What does this tell us?

These examples and others tell me the following: God foresees the needs, challenges or suitability of a particular era and appoints His servants to serve Him according to the characteristics, needs and challenges of that age. Having called these servants, He then uses the circumstances of their lives to train them for leadership. Thus we can say with Paul, "For he chose us in him before the creation of the world ..." (Ephesians 1:4). That is how important those of us called by the Lord are in His sight. He foresaw the need for our existence in our time before the creation of the world. Having thus chosen us, He uses the good and bad experiences we go through to shape our lives. He uses our parents and the people we interact with and relate to. He uses events, the era and place we are born in, the education process we go through, the training we undergo etc, to prepare us for leadership.

### The Third Principle: Giftedness: When God Calls us He Gives us Gifts and Talents

God does not call us to something that is completely beyond our ability. Giftedness goes hand in hand with the call to leadership. Upon each and every one of us who is called to leadership, God bestows certain gifts. Not only are we given gifts; we are called to utilize these gifts through a profession, career or vocation He has called us to follow (See Williams 2002:95). The following scripture passages explain this principle:

   a.  Romans 12: 6-8
   b.  1 Corinthians 12: 4-11; 28-31
   c.  Ephesians 4:7-11; 16

The first two are quoted here in full and the third in part:

   a.  "We have different gifts, according to the grace given
       to each of us. If your gift is prophesying, then

prophesy in accordance with your faith; if it is serving, then serve; if it is teaching, then teach; if it is to encourage, then give encouragement; if it is giving, then give generously; if it is to lead, do it diligently; if it is to show mercy, do it cheerfully." (Romans 12:6-8).

b.  "There are different kinds of gifts, but the same Spirit distributes them. There are different kinds of service, but the same Lord. There are different kinds of working, but in all of them and in everyone it is the same God at work.

Now to each one the manifestation of the Spirit is given for the common good. To one there is given through the Spirit a message of wisdom, to another a message of knowledge by means of the same Spirit, to another faith by the same Spirit, to another gifts of healing by that one Spirit, to another miraculous powers, to another prophecy, to another distinguishing between spirits, to another speaking in different kinds of tongues, and still to another the interpretation of tongues. All these are the work of one and the same Spirit, and he distributes them to each one, just as he determines" (1 Corinthians 12:4-11).

c.  "But to each one of us grace has been given as Christ apportioned it... So Christ himself gave the apostles, the prophets, the evangelists, the pastors and teachers, to equip his people for works of service, so that the body of Christ may be built up until we all reach unity in the faith and in the knowledge of the Son of God and become mature, attaining to the whole measure of the fullness of Christ... From him

the whole body, joined and held together by every
supporting ligament, grows and builds itself up in
love, as each part does its work" (Ephesians 4:7-11;
16).

Putting these passages side by side helps us to have more
clarity on the issue of gifts in the service of the Kingdom. In
the first passage, as in the other two, it becomes clear that we
are given different gifts – gifts of prophesy, serving, teaching,
leadership and so on. The emphasis is on the fact that whatever
gift you are given, make sure you use it optimally and with the
right attitude. Thus if your gift is to lead, lead diligently; if it is
to show mercy, do it cheerfully; if it is to give, give generously
etc.

The second passage tells us where these gifts come from:
They are distributed by the Spirit of Christ, the Holy Spirit. The
gifts are not meant for the one who receives them – but "for
the common good," for the body of Christ. An important
point that this passage reveals is that the Spirit distributes these
gifts "just as he determines." Some church leaders seem to
think that the gifts of the Holy Spirit are only given to those
who hold positions of authority, but this statement tells us the
Spirit can distribute gifts to those in high positions and to
ordinary members of the body of Christ. We are all important.
It is not only the Bishop, Pastor or Evangelist who is important
as we are all made worthy to receive the gifts of the Holy Spirit,
unworthy though we all are. This is also why it is important to
recognize that in the Church the citizens of the Kingdom are
called upon to play different roles: some as Apostles, some as
Prophets, some as Evangelists and some as Teachers, and so

on. Just as we are given different gifts, we are also called to different careers and responsibilities. There is therefore no room in the Church of Christ for envying either those in high positions or brothers and sisters who possess certain gifts. Each must be satisfied with the role allocated to him or her, but make sure they use the position and gifts optimally.

The third passage clarifies that all these vocations, these positions and gifts are meant to equip the people for the building up of the Church of Christ so that we all grow in unity and knowledge of the Son of God. The body of Christ is an organic structure made up of individual "supporting ligaments" that help it to grow and build itself "in love." Now, the body of Christ is able to do this "as each part does its work." This means that if any of us do not do the work they are called to do, the building of the body of Christ is negatively affected and the work of promoting the Kingdom of God on earth greatly suffers. We should remember that the keys to the Kingdom of heaven have been given to the Church (See Matthew 16:18-19). If the one who holds the keys to the Kingdom has been incapacitated, then it becomes difficult for others to find their way to the Kingdom.

These passages present a challenge to both the individual citizen in the transitional phase of the Kingdom and to the Church as the body of Christ. To the individual, the challenge is to understand one's gifting and utilise the gifts diligently for the development and effectiveness of the Church and the growth of the Kingdom of God on earth. On its part, the Church must recognise the gifts of its members, great and small, and encourage the members to be aware of their gifts and to use them effectively for the purpose of spreading the Kingdom of God on earth.

*Reluctance to Serve as a Result of Real or Imagined Lack of Gifts*

Sometimes we are tempted to hide behind what we consider to be our lack of relevant gifts and talents, or behind the absence of resources. We shall discuss below the issue of obedience to God when He calls us. At this point, it suffices to explain that when God calls us, and we have prayed about the call and are convinced the Lord has given us a mission, we should not hide behind the excuse of not having the relevant gift. When God sends us to work for the Kingdom, He will give us the means. The Bible has examples of servants of God who were tempted to refuse carrying out the mission the Lord had given them, because they thought they did not have the appropriate gifts or qualities. A good example is Prophet Jeremiah. When God called him, the prophet gave excuses: "Alas, Sovereign LORD," I said, "I do not know how to speak; I am too young." The Lord commanded him to go regardless, and promised him, "They will fight against you, but will not overcome you, for I am with you and will rescue you," the Lord declared to him (Jeremiah 1: 6-19).

Another good example is Moses. When the Lord called him to lead the Israelites out of Egypt, like Jeremiah after him, Moses gave excuses. This is one of them: 'Moses said to the LORD, "Pardon your servant, Lord. I have never been eloquent, neither in the past nor since you have spoken to your servant. I am slow of speech and tongue." Moses even went on to impudently say, "Pardon your servant, Lord. Please send someone else."' (See Exodus 4:10-13). This made the LORD angry, but He (the LORD) went on to demonstrate an important leadership principle. A good leader who knows he /she lacks some skills will surround himself/herself with supporters who possess such skills. In this case, the LORD told Moses his brother Aaron would assist him: "He will speak to the people for you, and it will be as if he were your mouth and as if you were God to him" (Exodus 4:16).

The moral here is this: when God has called us, and we have prayed about it and are convinced He is calling us, we should embark on the journey even if we think we do not have the talents and resources. This is what we learn from our father in Faith, Abraham, who set out to go to a country he did not know just because God had told him to.

### The Fourth Principle: The Lord often Tests Those He has Chosen

As already explained in an earlier chapter, God often tests those He has chosen (See Chapter 1). The tests may take different forms, but they are basically tests on obedience to God. Among the qualities being tested are the following: Are we willing to give up our own will and do God's will? Are we willing to surrender ourselves to God's will, in other words? Do we have faith in God's promises? Do we have the patience to let God help us achieve the particular task in His own time and in His own way? Are we willing to make sacrifices for the sake of God's mission? Referring to the actual experience that Muslim converts to Christianity are facing in some Islamic countries today, Tom Doyle (2015:203-204) challenges each one of us to answer the following questions which some of these converts have to ask themselves:

- Are you willing to suffer for Jesus?

# Learning to lead for the Kingdom

- Are you willing to die for Jesus?

Obeying God entails surrendering ourselves to His will. In *The Joy of Full Surrender*, Jean-Pierre de Caussade has explained that surrender to God's will is the essence of the prayer that Jesus taught us, the Lord's Prayer. This is a prayer we should say by both word and deed: "We repeat it vocally several times a day according to the teaching of God and His holy Church, but we utter it in the depth of our hearts each moment that we lovingly receive or suffer whatever is ordained by His venerable will" (de Caussade 1982:58). We pass the test of obedience when we choose to do His will as opposed to ours. As explained in earlier chapters, Jesus is the supreme example of this obedience to the Father. Scripture gives examples of other servants of God who passed the test in this way, and those who failed. The classic examples we could cite in this regard are our two fathers: the one may be called our father in the flesh, namely Adam, and the other is our father in faith, Abraham. Our focus here will be on these two.

Let us once again put the two tests side by side: Here is Adam's test: "And the LORD God commanded the man, 'You are free to eat from any tree in the garden; but you must not eat from the tree of the knowledge of good and evil, for when you eat from it you will certainly die.'"(Genesis 2:16-17). And this was Abraham's test: "Some time later God tested Abraham. He said to him, 'Abraham!' 'Here I am,' he replied. Then God said, 'Take your son, your only son whom you love –Isaac – and go to the region of Moriah. Sacrifice him there as a burnt offering on a mountain I will show you'" (Genesis 22:1-2).

# Understanding one's Purpose and God's Call

On the face of it, Adam's test was a relatively simple one: just to avoid eating from a particular tree. However, his failure to obey God had consequences of cosmic proportions: Humanity lost the Kingdom of God on earth. Abraham's test was an extremely painful one, as any parent can testify. It was not only the thought of seeing his son's life being ended, but he himself being responsible for taking his own son's life. Consider the pain he suffered thinking about this. But the Bible tells us, "Early the next morning Abraham got up and loaded his donkey. He took with him two of his servants and his son Isaac..." His full surrender to God's will is expressed in his response to Isaac when the latter asked him, "'The fire and the wood are here,' Isaac said, 'but where is the lamb for the burnt offering?' Abraham answered, 'God himself will provide the lamb for the burnt offering, my son.'" Thus, Abraham was letting God act and do as He willed with His own servant. He perfected his full surrender to God when "he reached out his hand and took the knife to slay his son".

The Lord himself recognised Abraham's full surrender when He said, "Now I know that you fear God, because you have not withheld from me your son, your only son." (See Genesis 22:3-14). When we refer to Abraham as our father in faith, we are not simply talking about how he believed in God, left his own country and became the father of a new nation that believed in God. We are talking about this full surrender, this obedience to God in the most trying and most challenging of situations, and this humble faith that trusts that God will have a way in the most difficult of situations, this child's faith that "God will provide." This complete reliance on God's will gives us the strength to go wherever the Lord leads us in complete submission to him. Abraham's obedience also reminds us about another obedient servant of the Lord, Job, who, on hearing the completely unexpected news that he had lost all his wealth and all his children, cried out: "The LORD gave and the LORD has taken away; may the name of the LORD be praised" (Job 1:21).

Sometimes the test is very painful, as in the case of Job. In Hebrews 12 we are told that God disciplines us just as our earthly fathers discipline us. But God's test and discipline have a nobler purpose: "... but God disciplines us for our good, in order that we may share in his holiness. No discipline seems pleasant at the time, but painful. Later on, however, it produces a harvest of righteousness and peace for those who have been trained by it" (Hebrews 12:10-11). This is precisely what happened to Job even in his earthly life: "After Job had prayed for his friends, the LORD restored his fortunes and gave him twice as much as he had before ... The LORD blessed the latter part of Job's life more than the former part" (Job 42:10-12). Some of the discipline entails physical suffering or illness; while some forms of discipline may entail problems of various kinds such as financial loss, rejection by others, and so on. The important thing is that we must try to pass the test in obedience to God our Father.

### Conclusion: How Great To Be Called!

Serious reflection on our calling should lead us to a greater appreciation of who we are as individuals. We are not just statics in God's plan of things. As an omnipotent Creator, God foresaw the needs and challenges of each age, and with that foresight, He foresaw the need for each one of us to fulfil His will and wish for our age. He then pre-arranged for each one of us to be in an environment in which we could grow and develop as leaders. That environment includes the kind of parents who bring us up, the education we receive, the challenges we face in life and so on. The Lord makes sure He provides for us by way of gifts, talents and people who surround us, some of whom will complement us where our abilities do not meet all the skills and qualities we need to fulfil our mission on earth.

So important is our mission in God's sight that He trains us for the task He has given us. That training includes some kind of test. Are we fit to help God accomplish His plan for our time, our age? It is not by our own power that we are able to accomplish our mission on earth and play our part in fulfilling God's plan for the age. To pass the test, entails being faithful to the One who has sent us into this world; it entails surrendering ourselves to Him and asking for His grace so that we may be fit to serve. What this also means is that we must reflect more on how we should respond to God's call. We discuss this matter in some detail in the next chapter.

Learning to lead for the Kingdom

# CHAPTER SEVEN

## Responding to God's Call to you...

*Understanding God's Ways of Calling His Messengers*

In the previous chapter, we discussed what God does with the messengers He has chosen – how He trains and equips them. In this chapter, we discuss how we should respond to His call. In order to discuss our response, we should first examine ways in which God calls us, the means He uses to draw our attention to the fact that He is calling us. In other words, how do you know that the Lord is calling you? We begin by looking at how God has called His servants in the past.

Throughout the history of salvation and the coming of the Kingdom, God has used different ways to call His messengers. In Old Testament times, right down to the time of the birth of Jesus, dreams were often a means used by God to speak to His chosen servants. Thus Joseph was sold by his brothers because he had dreamt dreams, and they called him "the dreamer." In Egypt he became well known as an interpreter of dreams and it was this gift that saved Egypt from the seven years of famine, and ironically saved Jacob's family from the devastating effects of the famine (See Genesis 37-47). The power to interpret

161

dreams was also given to Daniel (Daniel 2 ff). In the days of Jesus, the child was at least twice saved by dreams. The Magi were warned in a dream not to go back to Herod, and Joseph, Mary's husband, was told in a dream to flee to Egypt with the child and his mother (See Matthew 2: 12-15).

A common way in Old Testament times was some kind of physical presence often accompanied by a real voice. In calling Abraham, the Lord used an audible voice: 'The "LORD had said to Abram, "Go from your country, your people and your father's household to the land I will show you"' (Genesis 12:1). In addition to using His voice, the Lord seems to have sometimes appeared in a physical form to Abraham (See Genesis 17: 1-5).To Moses, God appeared in a burning bush and then called out, "Moses! Moses!" Amazingly, God went on to reveal His own identity to Moses, "I am the God of your father, the God of Abraham, the God of Isaac and the God of Jacob" (See Exodus 3:1-6). Similarly, Samuel heard the voice of God calling "Samuel!" and at first Samuel thought it was the priest Eli (See 1 Samuel 3:1-21). In the days of the great Prophets – Isaiah, Jeremiah and Ezekiel – powerful visions seem to have been a key factor in God's communication with His messenger (e.g. Isaiah 6:1-8; Ezekiel 1:4-28). Daniel was so gifted in visions that he was even shown the end times (See Daniel 12: 1-13).

To Mary, the Mother of Jesus, God sent the Angel Gabriel (e.g. Luke 1:26-38). The same Angel had appeared to Zechariah to convey God's message about the birth of John the Baptist (See Luke 1:11-25). When the Son of God walked the earth in human form, He personally called His disciples (See Luke 5: 1-

11). Saul (the Apostle Paul) had a dramatic experience in which He fell from a horse and heard Jesus calling Him (Acts 9:1ff).

In our day, some may be privileged to see God in a physical form – in the form of Jesus or an Angel or Mary. Some may be privileged to have the kind of Damascus experience that Saul had. That experience may not be in the kind of violent or forceful form like falling from a horse, but in the form of a sudden revelation like what happened to John Wesley (Wakefield 1990: 15-18), or to Mother Teresa (Mundakel 2003:20-25). For the most part, however, God uses the indwelling presence of the Holy Spirit to speak to us. This is the special gift that the followers of Jesus have that Paul explains in his First Letter to the Corinthians (See 1 Corinthians 2:6-16). In this regard, many of us will go through a process which is much slower and less dramatic than the experience of John Wesley and Mother Teresa, but the Holy Spirit will be guiding us. This needs further explanation.

### Jesus and the Holy Spirit in the Transitional Phase of the Kingdom

In comforting His disciples before His arrest, Jesus said, "I will not leave you as orphans; I will come to you" (John 14:18). And as He gave the Great Commission, His closing words were, "And surely I am with you always, to the very end of the age" (Matthew 28:20). The question could be asked, "How is Jesus with the citizens of the Kingdom in the transitional phase?" There are three ways in which Jesus assures us of His presence, and we summarize them here:

163

# Learning to lead for the Kingdom

First, we have His Word in the Bible. We must negate any suggestion that the Bible is just a history book in which we learn about the Man called Jesus, who lived two thousand years ago. Yes, figures like Abraham, Moses and John the Baptist can to some extent be regarded as historical figures, but what they represent is not just history. The Bible is God speaking to us now as He did in those ancient times. And when He spoke, Jesus did not only speak for the benefit of His twelve disciples. He is speaking the same words to us now, in our time. Just as He comforted His disciples in their distress about what was to happen to Him (See John 14), He speaks to us now, comforting us about our own distressful situations such as sickness, death of loved ones, oppression, rejection and other forms of suffering. The writing of this chapter has taken place during the time of the Corona Virus (COVID-19). This is an example of cases when believers should hear Jesus expressing concern about the problems of humanity. We are not orphans because He is with us always. We should learn to hear His comforting voice with the ears of faith. Sometimes we read a Scripture passage and we hear Jesus' voice addressing us through those pages of the Bible.

The second way may not be believed by some followers of Jesus; but for those who believe in "the real presence" in the Eucharist, Christ's presence is real. When such a believer walks down the aisle to go and receive Holy Communion, he/she meets Jesus with the eyes, mind and heart of faith. This is one way in which His words, "I will come to you" become realised. Reality is not only what we see with our physical eyes; what is unseen can be even more real than what is seen. As the Apostle Paul says, "So we fix our eyes not on what is seen, but on what is unseen, since what is seen is temporary, but what is unseen is eternal" (2 Corinthians 4:18). It was because he believed in "the real presence," that Paul could write, "For those who eat and drink *without discerning the body of Christ* eat and drink judgment on themselves" (1 Corinthians 11:29). The body of Christ in that consecrated piece of bread has to be *discerned* by the eyes and mind of faith. In Hebrews 11:3, we are told, "By faith we understand that the universe was formed at God's command, so that what is seen was not made out of what was visible." In the Eucharist, what is visible, namely, the bread and wine, represents the reality of the invisible body and blood of Christ that we do not see with our naked physical eyes.

The third way in which Jesus ensures we are not alone is what some authorities have called "the Spirit of Christ" (e.g. Murray 1984). We are referring here to the indwelling presence of the Holy Spirit. Prior to saying, "I will not leave you as orphans," Jesus makes this promise: "And I will ask the Father, and he will give you another advocate to help you and be with you forever – the Spirit of truth" (John 14:16-17a). Further on in the same discourse, Jesus says, "But the Advocate, the Holy Spirit, whom the Father will send in my name, will teach you all things and will remind you of everything I have said to you" (John 14:26). I quote these two Scripture verses to make two points: First, the Spirit of truth is with us *forever*. Second, the Holy Spirit not only teaches all things, but reminds us of everything Jesus said while He walked the earth. This is why we have the *New Testament,* and I refer in particular to the gospels. They were written after Jesus had gone back to the Father because the Holy Spirit inspired the evangelists to record what Jesus had said while He was still on earth.

# Learning to lead for the Kingdom

Andrew Murray (1984:7) makes an important distinction between the workings of the Holy Spirit in the Old Testament and how He works in the New Testament. In the Old Testament the Spirit came upon certain individuals and worked on them in a special way at special times. In the New Testament the Holy Spirit comes and dwells in people and works from within them. The phrase generally used is "the indwelling presence" of the Holy Spirit. This leads me to make a further distinction between the Old Testament and the New Testament: In the Old Testament, the voice of God we hear is predominantly that of God the Father. And often when He called, it was in an audible voice as explained above. In the New Testament, we have the words of Jesus in the gospels and the quiet voice of the Holy Spirit. It is as if God the Father has withdrawn to the background to allow the Son (through the Bible) and the Spirit to communicate His message to us.

I have called the Second Phase "the age of mature faith." This is because there is a greater demand made on us to use our faith to hear the voice of God within us. Abraham, Moses and the Prophets could actually hear God's audible voice. In our time, a passage in the Bible can strike us with a new freshness and make us realise a message we had not paid attention to before - as was the case with Mother Teresa, who experienced a revelation on one occasion in her understanding of the significance of Matthew 25: 31-43. In the case of the Holy Spirit, we must hear the voice within and *discern* God's message. This leads us to a discussion of the workings of the Holy Spirit and how He guides us in understanding God's call. A good starting point, is a passage from the Letter of the Apostle Paul to the Corinthians:

166

# Responding to God's Call to you...

"The Spirit searches all things, even the deep things of God. For who knows a person's thought except their own Spirit within them? In the same way no one knows the thoughts of God except the Spirit of God. What we have received is not the spirit of the world, but the Spirit who is from God, so that we may understand what God has freely given us. This is what we speak, not in words taught us by human wisdom but in words taught by the Spirit, explaining spiritual realities with Spirit-taught words" (1 Corinthians 2:10-13).

The Spirit teaches us all things. He enlightens us as we search for the will of God and seek to know our own mission in life. Furthermore, what the Lord wants of us, the Spirit will search and find for us. We will not only understand the gifts and graces God has given us; but the Spirit will also seek and reveal God's will for us. John Stott (2002:59 ff) has identified four workings of the Spirit that are summarised here:

- First, the Holy Spirit is the searching Spirit. He searches all things – even the deep things of God. He searches even the mind of God so that we may know what the Lord wants from us.
- The Holy Spirit is the revealing Spirit. In this regard, He reveals God's purpose for us.
- The Holy Spirit is an inspiring Spirit: He inspired the biblical authors to record the words of God, which words are true without error. In the context of this chapter, I wish to add that the Spirit inspires us to work for our calling in fulfilling the Father's mission for us.
- The Holy Spirit is the enlightening Spirit. He inspired the Apostles to write the Scriptures and enlightened

167

# Learning to lead for the Kingdom

their hearers and readers to understand the words used by the Apostles. The Holy Spirit therefore works at both ends – inspiring the authors and enlightening the readers to understand the Word. We as readers of the Bible are enlightened by the Holy Spirit.

These four are not the only ways the Holy Spirit works. Very importantly, He gives us power to proclaim the Kingdom of God. This is something we shall discuss in some detail in a later chapter. Our focus here, is on how the Spirit guides us to the mission the Father has ordained for us. I will begin by giving three examples:

a.  A young man's attention was drawn to a group of Methodists who were proclaiming the word of God as they went along singing in an African township in Johannesburg. The young man was so attracted by the group that he followed them. By the time he narrated this story, he was a Superintendent of the Methodist Church.

b.  A Catholic parish priest once told his parishioners about his own experience: He was a medical student at the University of the Western Cape in South Africa and was doing very well academically. But he heard this voice within him that kept on nagging him saying something to the effect that he was following the wrong profession; he ought to study for the priesthood. One day he made an irreversible decision. He packed his bags and went to his Bishop in a very different part of the country. He told his Bishop he wanted to study for the priesthood. He then went to the relevant seminary and was eventually ordained a priest, and, in his own words, "I have never looked back".

# Responding to God's Call to you...

c. My wife and I were teaching pastoral leadership to a group of seminarians who were close to completing their studies for the priesthood. Among them was one who was very visibly different from the rest. He was much older than the rest and happened to be the only one who was White in a class of Black seminarians. We were curious to know why he had decided to study for the priesthood at such an advanced age. He told us that he had actually been a seminarian much earlier at a young age. At some point, he decided to leave the seminary to pursue other interests. He worked for years in a secular environment. Then the thought of becoming a priest began to nag him again. He ultimately decided to abandon his job and return to the seminary as a mature student.

These examples tell us something about the workings of the Holy Spirit in our time. He dwells in us and reveals the will of God for us in different ways and inspires us to follow the path the Lord has chosen for us. For some the path may be straightforward, but for some others the path may be a winding one. Some hear the call when they are young; while others may not be aware of their real mission in life until much later in life. The examples given above are all about people called to serve God as religious people, but we are not all called to religious life, nor is being a Pastor, Priest or Nun the only way to proclaim the Kingdom. The vast majority of people are called to serve in non-religious professions such as teaching, the medical field, scientific research, politics etc. A good example of serving humanity in a field other than religious life is that of Alexander Fleming whose life is told in Chapter 8 of *Learning to Lead for a Better World.* Some may in fact be attracted to religious life while they are young, only to find out later God is calling them to a very different way of life. But whatever profession or way of life is ordained for us, the requirement for followers of Jesus is to proclaim the Kingdom and help to advance it in whatever sphere of life we are called to serve. With this background, we can now discuss guidelines on how to respond to God's call.

## Indicators for One's Call

You may ask, how then can I know that the Holy Spirit is guiding me to the mission that the Lord has ordained for me in this phase of the Kingdom, when it is not usual to hear God's loud voice, or to see a vision or to have an Angel sent to one? And how do I respond to God? There are several signs, what I have called "Indicators", meaning "Guides."

## First Indicator: Follow the Promptings of the Holy Spirit and Hear God's Voice

Normally, when God calls you to a particular vocation or ministry, you know it. You will feel it in the very marrow of your bones. The particular calling is what will excite you; you will feel drawn to it; and other professions will be of no interest to you, no matter how prestigious, enriching or even holy they may seem. It is the Holy Spirit prompting you. Jesus ascended to heaven two thousand years ago. The Holy Spirit first came to the Apostles on Pentecost Day (See Acts 2:1-13). But today, He comes to those born of water and the Spirit, who are God's temple in whom the Spirit dwells (See 1 Corinthians 3:16-17). He is the Spirit of truth who Jesus said will guide us into all the truth (See John 16:13). Usually, when you hear His voice in this way, He is guiding you into the truth of your calling.

On the other hand, you may be one of those for whom the call is at first unclear. In this regard, it may take a long time for you to come to a realisation of what God wants you to do in life. Whatever the case may be, you will have an inclination to do something, an inclination to serve God or humanity in a certain way; and that is an indication of the indwelling presence of the Holy Spirit within you. In secular parlance, this is referred to as *intuition* – the feeling that something is right, or that a certain course of action is the correct one when there is no real evidence that you are right; you just feel it. I divide intuition into two categories: natural intuition and divinely inspired intuition. Natural intuition is what every human being is capable of having. Divinely inspired intuition is a result of the workings of the Holy Spirit. Here the Holy Spirit is working as the revealing Spirit, directing us to the mission God has ordained for us.

However long it may take to come, you will arrive at that Aha! moment, the Eureka moment when your purpose in life becomes clear. There will come that time for the individual who is searching for God's will when the words spoken to the people of Zion by the Prophet ring true: 'Whether you turn to the right or to the left, your ears will hear a voice behind you, saying, "This is the way; walk in it"' (Isaiah 30:21).

***Second Indicator: The Gifts You Have Are Often an Indication of What God Wants You to Do with Your Life***

# Learning to lead for the Kingdom

We have learnt the principle that when God calls us for leadership, He gives us gifts. God will not call us to do something that is completely beyond our ability. He wants us to have a sense of fulfilment as we perform our functions in His service, and this entails doing something we enjoy doing; something we have abilities for. Rick Warren (2002:244) has rightly pointed out that the gifts you do have are "clues to knowing God's will for you." Ask yourself therefore: Do I have the abilities for the ministry or vocation to which I think God is calling me? You may have certain shortcomings. These may be taken care of by taking relevant courses or undergoing some kind of training. Such shortcomings do not necessarily indicate inabilities; they may just be the result of insufficient training.

## Third Indicator: Does Your Intuition (Inclination) Pass the Test of Double Confirmation?

Double Confirmation is a term invented by Dr J. Robert Clinton in *The Making of a Leader*. He defines it as "the unusual guidance PROCESS ITEM in which God makes clear His will by reinforcing it through more than one source, each source independent of the others." (Clinton 1988:239). The Bible gives a number of examples of double confirmation:

A fascinating example is that of Mary visiting her cousin Elizabeth. The Angel Gabriel had said to Mary, "Greetings, you who are highly favoured! The Lord is with you." After a brief discussion with the Angel, Mary concluded the conversation with these words: "'I am the Lord's servant,'" Mary answered, "May your word to me be fulfilled."'(See Luke 1:26-38).

When Mary greets Elizabeth on her arrival at the home of the latter, Elizabeth in a loud voice echoes the words of both the angel and Mary, "Blessed are you among women, and blessed is the child you will bear!" She concludes her response to Mary with these words: "Blessed is she who has believed that the Lord would fulfil His promises to her!" (Luke 1:39-45). To Mary, Elizabeth's greeting was a confirmation of the conversation between her and the Angel Gabriel; hence she burst into the wonderful response, the *Magnificat* (See Luke 1: 46-55).On his part, Clinton cites a number of examples such as the case of the conversion of Saul (Paul) and the message of Ananias (See Acts 9:1-19), and that of Peter and Cornelius (See Acts 10:1-8).

Clinton comments that double confirmation is not the kind of guidance God will use for the majority of decisions we make, but that a leader who is facing an important decision can ask God for this kind of intervention. In my view, double confirmation can also be used to clarify the way forward in a case where one is not sure about the decision they want to make. I can cite the case of one of our children who, as he was about to finish high school and was preparing to go to university, was not at all clear about what he wanted to specialise in. One of the areas he was entertaining was Medicine. It so happened that one of our Church friends was the Superintendent of a hospital. We asked him to arrange for our son to work at the hospital during one of his school holidays. The Superintendent enthusiastically agreed to the plan.

As an intern, our son experienced what working in a hospital was like: Among other things he saw badly wounded people being admitted and he being required to help; he saw very sick people and saw some dying. What he saw and experienced was far from pleasing to him. When he came back home, his comment was, "Mummy and Daddy, I still don't know what I want to specialise in; but if there is anything I now know I don't want to be, it is to be a doctor." His natural intuition had told him, he is called to serve society as a doctor, but the inclination failed the test of double confirmation. Today, he is a successful accountant and auditor.

### Fourth Indicator: Do You Learn Lessons from Biblical and Other Christian Role Models?

The Bible presents us with examples of how to respond and how not to respond to God. We have the example of Abraham who just did what the Lord commanded him to do – whether it was to leave his own country and family and go to a new country (See Genesis 12); or whether it was to sacrifice his son as a burnt offering (See Genesis 22). In this regard, Abraham foreshadows Jesus Christ. Jesus left heaven to come down to earth to dwell with us human beings. Abraham was about to sacrifice his son of the promise, Isaac; and Jesus, the Son of God, sacrificed his own life on the cross for the sake of humanity in obedience to His Father. The model of obedience to God in both cases, is one that should help to guide us when the Lord presents difficult situations to us. To these examples, we should add Mary's surrender to God in her response, "I am the Lord's servant; May your word to me be fulfilled" (Luke 1:38).

We have the example of Moses and Jeremiah who at first resisted God's call saying they were not capable of carrying out what He wanted them to do: After God had explained everything to Him and showed Him miraculous signs, Moses still had the stubbornness to say, "Pardon your servant, Lord. Please send someone else" (Exodus 4:13). Jeremiah gave his young age and lack of eloquence as excuses: "'Alas, Sovereign LORD,' I said, "I do not know how to speak; I am too young'" (Jeremiah 1:6). In contrast to these initial responses of Moses and Jeremiah, we have Isaiah's answer to the Lord: 'Then I heard the voice of the Lord saying, "Whom shall I send? And who will go for us?" And I said, "Here am I. Send me!"'" (Isaiah 6:8).

A very unique and interesting case is that of Samuel, whose mother, Hannah, had offered him to the Lord under the priest Eli. Samuel was a very young boy, working for the Lord under Eli. One night, Samuel heard his name being called, and he ran to the priest who was lying down in his sleeping place in the house of the Lord, and said "Here I am; you called me." The priest told him, "I did not call; go back and lie down." This happened three times and Eli realised it was the Lord calling the boy. Eli told the boy how to respond if he heard the voice again. So, when for the fourth time the Lord called, "Samuel! Samuel!" Samuel answered, "Speak, for your servant is listening." Clearly, Eli was both a divine contact and a mentor for Samuel. Not only was he mentoring the boy Samuel in the house of God; he also became the interpreter of God's voice for Samuel, and he taught Samuel the appropriate way to respond to God. The fourth time Samuel heard the Lord call was in the nature of double confirmation

This item is more of a guide than an indicator. It is only an indicator to the extent that one can intuitively, by divine intuition, hear the voice of God calling, in which case, the call becomes identical with Indicator 1 – the promptings of the

Holy Spirit. This would be the case with the majority of us. There may be a few who have received the special gift of actually hearing the physical voice of the Lord, but there are not many such in this second phase of the Kingdom. Choo Thomas (2006) has written a whole book about her fascinating experience of not only hearing the voice of Jesus, but of actually being shown heaven by the Lord. What is more important for the rest of us, is that the Biblical examples we have given instruct us in regard to how to respond to God. In the responses of Abraham and Mary, we learn the principle of full surrender to the will of God. God is the potter and we are the clay; when we are convinced He is calling us we should let Him do whatever He wants us to do for Him. In the examples of Moses and Jeremiah, we learn that the anointed of God can discuss with the Lord to seek clarification. Even Mary found it necessary to ask, "How will this be, since I am a virgin?" (Luke 1:34). So, if one genuinely feels in their heart that there is something in the call of God which sounds problematic, they should pray and seek clarification from the Lord. What would be wrong is after it has become clear what the call is to then answer like Moses, "Please send someone else." Or like Jeremiah, "I am too young."

In the responses of Isaiah and Samuel, we have other examples of how to respond to the Lord when the call is clear. Even in our own time, Jesus is saying, "The harvest is plentiful, but the workers are few. Ask the Lord of the harvest, therefore, to send out workers into his harvest field." (Luke 10:2). If we hear the voice of the Lord saying, "Whom shall I send?" we should be ready to respond like Isaiah, "Here am I. Send me!" Or if the message is not yet clear, we should pray quietly in our hearts and answer like Samuel, "Speak, Lord, for your servant is listening." There is something further we learn from Samuel: It is good to have a mentor. When the Lord calls, it helps to discuss our sense of divinely inspired intuition with a senior and more experienced Pastor, Priest, Nun or Teacher. His/her contribution can lead to very useful insights or clarity of purpose and mission.

Finally, this indicator is an invitation to us to read the Bible: The Bible is God talking to us. As citizens of the Kingdom we must be in the habit of reading the Bible in order to grow both spiritually and as messengers of the Lord. When we feel the Lord is calling us to a vocation or ministry, we should learn more about how we should fulfil the requirements of our mission and about how to respond to God by listening to the voice of the Spirit speaking to us through the Scriptures. Reading about Christian role models who answered the call of God in our time and other post apostolic eras can also help to inspire us.

# Learning to lead for the Kingdom

# CHAPTER EIGHT

## The Obligation and Power to Proclaim the Kingdom

### *The Task for Kingdom Citizens of the 21ˢᵗ Century*

Chapter 5 ends with a series of questions the followers of Jesus should ask themselves in respect of their obligations as citizens of the Kingdom. Every one of these questions is important, but for our purposes in this chapter, we shall begin by reminding ourselves of the following commands and statements. The fourth one is not part of the original series:

1. "All authority in heaven and on earth has been given to me. Therefore, go and make disciples of all nations, baptizing them in the name of the Father and of the Son and of the Holy Spirit, and teaching them to obey everything I have commanded you. And surely I am with you always, to the very end of the age" (Matthew 28: 18-20).

2. "You did not choose me, but I chose you so that you might go and bear fruit – fruit that will last – and so that whatever you ask in my name the Father will give you" (John 15:26).

179

# Learning to lead for the Kingdom

3. 'Then they gathered around him and asked him, "Lord, are you at this time going to restore the kingdom to Israel?"

   He answered them: "It is not for you to know the times or dates the Father has set by his own authority. But you will receive power when the Holy Spirit comes on you; and you will be my witnesses in Jerusalem, and in all Judea and Samaria, and to the ends of the earth" (Acts 1:6-8).

4. "And this gospel of the kingdom will be preached in the whole world as a testimony to all nations, and then the end will come" (Matthew 24:14).

These passages present both the challenge facing the followers of Jesus as well as the means by which to tackle the challenge. In the second passage our Lord and Master commands us to bear fruit, and fruit that will last. There may have been times when the Christian Church was very effective in proclaiming the Kingdom, but has that been sustained? How productive are we, the Christians of our time, in comparison to, say, the early Christians, in witnessing for Jesus? We could measure our productivity using the parameters given in the Parable of the Bags of Gold (See Matthew 25:14-30) and the Parable of the Ten Minas (See Luke 19:11-27).

If we care enough to assess the work we are doing, our productivity in preaching the news and helping to build the Kingdom of God on earth, could we say, we compare fairly with the servant who received five bags of gold and produced five more, or with the one who hid his bag and produced no fruit? Are we like the servant who was given a mina and produced ten more, or like the one who kept his mina laid away

# The Obligation and Power to Proclaim the Kingdom

in a piece of cloth and produced no profit at all? Or could we, perhaps, console ourselves and say, we compare very well with the servant who was given two bags and produced two more, or the servant in Luke who produced five minas? Whatever our response may be, the time has come for the followers of Jesus to realize that these parables are not just stories, but messages to believers to obey the Lord's commands. Often when we read the parables or hear them read to us by our Priests and Pastors, we tend to think they are directed at other people, and not at ourselves. We might even think these were directives to the Apostles, and not to us. Furthermore, as suggested in Chapter 5, we sometimes forget that the challenges Jesus presents apply to us both individually and collectively. The challenge is both to the Church in its various denominations and to the individual disciple of Jesus.

Some might ask: How can we assess our performance? What measurement do we use to see whether our performance is as it should be or not? Well, the answer is in these scripture quotations. The Lord made sure He gave us parameters by which to measure our performance and our commitment to His commands: We find these parameters in passages 1, 3 and 4. Passage 1 commands us to "go and make disciples of *all nations.*" Passage 3 requires of us to be witnesses of Jesus, not only in Jerusalem, Judea and Samaria, but "to the ends of the earth." If we are genuinely praying for the reign of Christ to come, then we must pay attention to passage 4. The end of the world will come when the gospel of the Kingdom has been preached "in the whole world" and "as a testimony to all nations." To what extent have we done all this? Have we preached the gospel to all nations as commanded by the Lord in passage 1 and passage 4?

To see the gravity of the challenge from a 21st Century perspective, let us look at some statistics: The total population of the world in 2020 is estimated to be 7.8 billion people. Of these 2.4 billion are Christians, constituting about 29.81% of the world population. The following are comparative 2019 figures with a few other big religious groups (from the Pew Research Center):

| *Religion* | *Adherents* | *Percentage* |
|---|---|---|
| Christianity | 2.4 billion | 29.81% |
| Islam | 1.9 billion | 24.60% |
| Secular/Non-religious/Agnostics | 1.2 billion | 14.28% |
| Hinduism | 1.15 billion | 13.91% |

These figures show that Christianity is still the largest group in the world, but predictions are that this will change in this very century. *Fact Tank* (2017) has published an article which predicts that by 2060 Muslims will most likely surpass Christians as the world's largest religious group. On the same subject, *The Two-Way* has published a report that suggests that Islam will nearly equal Christianity by 2050 and eclipse it by 2070. The increase of secularism is a key factor in determining the future of Christianity. Significantly, the figures above show that people of no religious affiliation including agnostics now number 1.2 billion, which is 50% of the Christian population and the same figure as Catholics who are considered the largest Christian group. A major factor in the rising of this group is

# The Obligation and Power to Proclaim the Kingdom

apostasy, the abandoning of Christianity by nations that were once Christian, which is the case with many Western countries today. I make this last point to show the magnitude of the problem of secularism in our time, which is an indication of the extent to which religion has ceased to have any meaning in people's lives.

It could be argued that we should not be overly concerned with number crunches. The Lord may not have suggested that Christianity should necessarily be the largest religion. Be that as it may, the challenge is still real from whatever angle we look at it. We have an obligation to ask these questions and answer them:

- Have we made disciples of all nations?
- Have we been witnesses of Jesus "to the ends of the earth?"
- Have we preached the Gospel of the Kingdom in the whole world?
- To these we need to add the other questions raised at the end of Chapter 5, and then ask ourselves "Have we borne fruit that lasts?"

### The Source of the Power to Proclaim the Kingdom

Citizens of the Kingdom have a duty to spread the good news of the Kingdom of God. But by what authority do they do this? And where do they get the power to preach the Gospel to the whole world? The authority is given in passage 1 (See Matthew 28:16-20) and passage 3 (See Acts 1:8). The power is granted in the Acts passage: "But you will receive power when the Holy Spirit comes on you; and you will be my witnesses in

# Learning to lead for the Kingdom

Jerusalem, and in all Judea and Samaria, and to the ends of the earth." This was confirmation of what Jesus had said in His promise of the Holy Spirit (See John 14:15-18, 26; 15:26-27; 16:13-14). And indeed on the day of Pentecost, all the Apostles were filled with the Holy Spirit and began to speak in other tongues (See Acts 2).

With the power of the Spirit, Peter stood up and began to give bold testimony about Jesus. On the same day, three thousand converts were baptized and added to the number of the disciples, and the Church was born! From that time on, the Church began to grow and spread rapidly. Fierce persecution of believers also arose with Stephen becoming the first martyr (See Acts 7:54-60). Saul, who had been present when Stephen was stoned and had approved of the murder, became a leading activist of the persecution. But with his conversion, the faith spread rapidly to the gentiles (See Acts 9 ff). There are two points to note here: The Church was born when the Holy Spirit had descended on the Apostles and given them power and courage to witness for Jesus and proclaim the Kingdom of God. Second, the birth of the Church was not an easy and pleasant process. The believers suffered for their belief in Jesus and the Kingdom. As we follow the account of the Acts, we realize that growing the Church was hard work. It was not a walk in the park.

Andrew Murray (1984:56) has this desire: That all prayers for the guidance of the Holy Spirit have this as their aim: "Power to witness for Christ and do effective service in conquering the world for Him." If we are to be witnesses of Christ to the ends of the earth in our time, we must have the power of the Holy Spirit. Jesus did what He did, fearlessly proclaiming the Kingdom and performing miracles, because

# The Obligation and Power to Proclaim the Kingdom

from the time of His baptism, He was filled with the Holy Spirit. For us to get guidance on what to do about the Kingdom in the light of the discussion in the previous section of this chapter, we must also be filled with the Holy Spirit. In a previous chapter, we learned about the Holy Spirit as the enlightening Spirit and revealing Spirit. Faced with what appears to be a major crisis for the followers of Jesus in the twenty-first century, we should pray to the Holy Spirit to reveal the will of the Father for us in our time, to enlighten us about how to respond to the challenges we are facing and then give us the power to proclaim the Kingdom as we should.

All too often our prayer to the Holy Spirit seems too intellectual; we ask for the Spirit in too much of an intellectual fashion without giving ourselves time to reflect and invite the Spirit so that He can possess us and use us for the Father's mission. Perhaps Paul's message to the Ephesians is appropriate for us in the twenty-first century when He said about his prayer to the Father: "I pray that out of his glorious riches he may strengthen you with power through his Spirit in your inner being, so that Christ may dwell in your hearts through faith" (Ephesians 3: 16-17). In other words, with Christ dwelling in our hearts, we should be able to experience a new Pentecost and be empowered by the Spirit to witness for Jesus with the kind of bravery that Peter showed on the day of Pentecost.

What seems to be a precondition for experiencing this new Pentecost, is giving ourselves and surrendering ourselves to the Spirit so that He can use His power to rule in us. Andrew Murray (1984:60) has wisdom to share in this regard: "Unconditional submission and obedience to the power in our inner life is the one condition for our being clothed with it." This entails having a real encounter with the Spirit, not just an intellectual thought or reflection. When we have this real encounter with the Spirit and are clothed with His power, we will have the power to help others to encounter God. Bill Johnson (2019:40) has said, "Living a life filled with the Spirit of God is the only possible way I can consistently bring others into an encounter with God."

For the world to encounter God, it should see God in us. The people of the world should see a difference between us and the rest of humanity. There should be something striking about us. For us to have this impact on the world, we must ourselves encounter God. We must be a people with such deep faith, people who are so obedient to the commands of Jesus our Lord and Master that God will come to dwell in us. As Jesus said, "Anyone who loves me will obey my teaching. My Father will love them, and we will come to them and make our home with them"(John 14:23). When the Father and Son have come to dwell in us, we will be able to manifest God: "Our greatest treasure is God Himself," says Bill Johnson, "Our greatest privilege is to manifest Him" (Johnson 2019:19). When we are able to manifest God, praying humbly and sincerely for guidance, the Holy Spirit, the Spirit of truth, the enlightening, revealing and inspiring Spirit, will show us the way and give us the power to proclaim the Kingdom of God to an unbelieving world.

If we are to proclaim the Kingdom, we must ourselves hunger and thirst for the Kingdom, we must surrender ourselves fully and completely to the requirements of the Kingdom so much so that it becomes our priority number one: "But seek first his kingdom and his righteousness, and all these

# The Obligation and Power to Proclaim the Kingdom

things will be given to you as well" (Matthew 6:33). Even the desire to proclaim the Kingdom must take second place to our hunger for the Kingdom of God. When the Kingdom has become our priority number one, the power to proclaim it will also be given to us. It is when the people of the world notice that while we are *in* this world, we are not *of* this world, that they will pay attention to our message of the Kingdom. This is not to say the world will necessarily love us. Some may even hate us and persecute us for manifesting God and proclaiming the Kingdom. Jesus warned us: "If the world hates you, keep in mind that it hated me first. If you belonged to the world, it would love you as its own" (John 15:18-25). Precisely because we will show that we are not of this world, we will be persecuted by some. However, the world will notice that we are different, and some will hear and follow the Word.

### *How the Early Christians Suffered and Conquered*

This chapter challenges us to invite the Spirit to possess us so that we can effectively proclaim the Kingdom of God in the modern world. We have just seen above that Andrew Murray suggests that all prayers for guidance by the Holy Spirit should have this aim: "Power to witness for Christ and do effective service in conquering the world for Him." In the face of the facts explained above, it may be justifiable to ask: Is this a doable job? This is perhaps the appropriate time to briefly look back to the golden age of Christianity to remind ourselves of how the disciples became powerful witnesses of Christ. We have already seen in this chapter that the birth of the Church came about as a result of the Holy Spirit manifesting Himself in the Apostles and giving them power to have the courage to boldly witness for Jesus. As the Church grew, the followers of Jesus became noticeable as a community. On the one hand, their behaviour and love for one another was so exemplary that people are reported to have commented, "See how these Christians love one another!" On the other hand, their determination and power to witness for Christ invited the wrath of both Jewish authorities and secular Roman authorities, and great persecution arose with many disciples losing their lives for Christ's sake. Subsequently, persecution appears to have been perpetrated from time to time by Roman emperors, some of whom issued directives to be worshipped. The first major persecution by the Romans occurred in Rome in year 64 under Emperor Nero, and that is when Peter was crucified and Paul beheaded (Bellito 2008:19). (Paul could not be subjected to crucifixion because he was a Roman citizen.) There were times when it was a crime to worship the Christian God to the extent the followers of Jesus worshipped underground in catacombs.

The first phase of victory seems to have come during the apostolic times, during the reign of Emperor Tiberius. The great historian Eusebius reports how the Emperor Tiberius, during whose reign the name Christian became known in the world of the time, favoured the doctrine, and communicated to the Senate in Rome that Christians should not be persecuted. Eusebius (Williamson 1965:39) reports on the positive impact of the Emperor's decision when "In every town and village, like a well-filled threshing floor, churches shot up bursting with eager members." He records how by the power of Christ and the teaching of His followers, people were freed from idol worship. He continues, "Thy turned their

# The Obligation and Power to Proclaim the Kingdom

backs on devilish polytheism in all its forms and acknowledged that there was one God only, the Fashioner of all things." But this state of affairs was not to last for long. Bellito (Ibid 20 ff) reports that more systematic persecution occurred from 193 to 305, with the so-called "great" persecution starting in 303 under Emperor Diocletion who carried out such acts as firing Christians from public service, destroying Churches and confiscating Scriptures.

Bellito reports: "In 201, converting to Judaism or Christianity was declared a capital offense, but the more the Romans killed Christians, the more Christianity grew." So, apparently the Church grew even despite Diocletion's edicts and activities. His successor, Emperor Galerius, was one of those who did not only persecute Christians, but went to the extreme extent of declaring that every Christian must sacrifice to the pagan Roman gods *or die*. As things turned out, it was the same Galerius who on his deathbed in 311 issued an edict of toleration for Christians and declared it lawful to worship the Christian God. The great moment came in 313 when Emperor Constantine issued the Edict of Milan which effectively declared Christianity the established religion of the Empire. In 380 and 381 Christianity was made the only religion of the Empire by Emperor Theodosius. Eusebius (Williamson 1965:304-305) describes the joy of Christians following the Edict of Milan in words whose mood I can only try to capture as follows:

*People everywhere were freed from the oppression they had suffered under despotic rulers. Freed from their miseries they now affirmed their faith in the one true God, the Defender of the godly. For those like Eusebius who had pinned all their hope on Christ, there was unspeakable joy as they saw how the places that had been brought to ruin by the oppressors were now coming back to life. The towers of cathedrals were once again beginning to pierce the skies, displaying a beauty and grandeur far greater than that of churches that had been destroyed by the despotic rulers.*

What is the point of this brief account? First, we should note that the establishment and growth of the early Church was a result of the power of the Holy Spirit. Second, having been given the power to witness for Christ and the Kingdom of God, men and women of the apostolic and sub-apostolic era, dedicated themselves to the task of preaching the Gospel and growing the Church under the most cruel, trying and dangerous circumstances. Third, not only were these trying circumstances; many lost their lives for the cause. It is worth noting that the martyrs were not only people who were highly placed in the structures of the Church. Among ordinary lay people, we have the examples of St Agnes, St Perpetua and St Felicity. It is also interesting to note that the second and third of these were from North Africa, and that St Felicity was a slave girl who managed to convert her own Madame, Perpetua, to the truth of the Christian faith. The fourth and final point is that Jesus said His followers should bear fruit. In this regard, there is no doubt that the Christians of the first three centuries bore fruit that lasted. Under the most difficult circumstances they spread the news of the Kingdom to the rest of the then known world. Of course, we know the world is much larger than their world, but in our time, the world has shrunk in terms of communication and travel; there is no part of this earth that we are unable to reach electronically, physically and by means of the printed word. But can we say we have taken the word to the ends of the earth when the population of Christians is 2.4 billion out of the total world population of 7.8 billion?

# The Obligation and Power to Proclaim the Kingdom

## *The Greatest Threat to Christianity is Christianity*

The early Christians spread the good news of the Gospel in the face of a powerful and hostile pagan state. What are the odds against us today? Many of us are practising the faith in what are considered democratic states where there is freedom of worship. But some are in states that seek to control and direct religion such as China. In such states, freedom of worship is restricted. Some are in states that are inimical to Christianity, such as Islamic states. In some such states, it may be very difficult to openly practice one's faith. All in all, it is reasonable to argue that in our time the greatest threats to the growth of the Kingdom of God as preached by Jesus can be identified as the following:

- Competing religions, in particular Islam
- Competing political ideologies as in states like China
- The growth and spread of secularism
- The disunity of Christians and the ever increasing denominations
- Lukewarm and nominal Christianity.

The last mentioned is one of the worst enemies of the Kingdom. Lukewarm and nominal Christians are not distinguishable from the rest of humanity. Perhaps the most positive things we do include running hospitals, institutions, charity organisations and engaging in other humanitarian activities. These are perhaps the most positive signs of manifesting the Kingdom of God in our time. The major sign that distinguishes the majority of us Christians from the rest of humanity is that we go to church on Sunday. But what are we doing more than others in that? Do others not go to their mosques, synagogues and temples on specific days every week? In the workplace, there is very little that shows that one is a Christian. Our behaviour, conduct and practices are the same as those of everybody else. In politics we simply go by the policy and practices of whatever political party we belong to. Our business practice is no different from what others do. Furthermore, many Christians are not aware of their responsibility to preach the gospel to those who do not know Jesus. Choo Thomas (2006: 193) quotes Jesus as saying, in part: "Only 20% of Churches are putting *Me* first... Many churches are not concerned about reaching out to lost souls at all. That is the most important thing for me."

If we add to the above the fact that Christians are so hopelessly divided, and that more and more new churches continue to come up, some for motives that do not seem spiritual, then it becomes clear that trying to identify the Kingdom of God with the Christian Church is problematic. By doing that we are, among other things, suggesting that the Kingdom of God is a sinful Kingdom, one in which in its second phase there is often no clear distinction between its own values and the values of the Kingdom of Satan which Jesus came to deliver us from. As noted earlier, there was a time when progress seemed to be on the cards in terms of bringing Christians together through the ecumenical movement, and no doubt, efforts are being made at high levels in bringing different Churches closer together, as will be referred to later; but a Catholic prelate, Cardinal Walter Kasper (2003:193-197), refers to two documents, one Catholic (*Dominus Iesus*) and the other Protestant (*Church Fellowship in Protestant Understanding*) which, to the mind of a lay Christian,

# The Obligation and Power to Proclaim the Kingdom

seem to wind the clock backwards in terms of Churches working together. In view of these developments, and though this may sound blasphemous, it is probably true to say that while competing religions and ideologies as well as the growth of secularism present a threat to Christianity *as a religion*, the greater threat to the Kingdom of God in our time is the state and nature of Christianity. Our first concern should not be numbers and the competition from other religions and ideologies, but the kind of Christianity we practice and project to the world. What picture of Christianity do we portray to the world? While we must at all times make sure that we project the correct theology and doctrine, what will draw people's attention to us is the kind of people we are: How do we relate to one another? How do we treat other people? What is our work ethic? How different are we from non-believers, from Muslims, from people of various other religions? Can other people distinguish Christians from the rest by the way they conduct themselves in various situations, whether it be in the work place, in business or in community projects, etc?

In support of my argument here, I might refer the reader to my second booklet published in 2001 (Ngara 2001b) in which I summarise the views of a Marxist admirer of Jesus, who thought what Christianity was in the 20th century compared to the ideals on which it was founded. Here I can only refer to three ideas that form part of his picture of Christianity as he saw it then (Ngara 2001b:75 ff):

1. Milan Machovec (1976) suggests the disproportion between the ideals which brought Christianity into existence and what it has become is, in his own

words, "to put it mildly, shocking." This, he says, should disturb Christians more than it does.

2. As part of his comment, he suggests we Christians might appeal to people by presenting a message in which we could, among other things, "Convince a person to rise above himself, to become different, to transform himself within, to begin to move by his own efforts towards the 'Kingdom of God' and so to belong to it" (Machovec 1976:88-89).

3. While I thought these were remarkable words coming from an avowed Marxist of the 1970s, I went on to refer to what he said were the qualities of Jesus as a man who embodied what he taught. I will come back to these comments shortly.

In the field of quality assurance, we talk of two main indicators of positive development: *qualitative* and *quantitative* development. Earlier on we quoted Bellito (2008) saying, "But the more the Romans killed Christians, the more Christianity grew." This talks to the quality of Christians who lived in that era. The quantitative growth of Christianity depended on the quality of believers who followed Christ in those times – on the extent of their commitment to Jesus, on the depth of their faith in the risen Christ and how they related to one another and to others. The question to ask is "*Why*" so? Perhaps the answer is in the origins of the word "Christians" or the Greek word *Christianoi*. As already noted, it was at Antioch that the disciples were first called Christians (See Acts 11:26). In the second chapter of Acts we read "Everyone was filled with awe at the many wonders and signs performed by the Apostles" (Acts 2:43). We are further told this about the fellowship of all

# The Obligation and Power to Proclaim the Kingdom

believers in Jerusalem: "They broke bread in their homes and ate together with glad and sincere hearts, praising God and enjoying the favour of all the people" (Acts 2:46-47). In *Come, Follow Me* (Ngara 2001a:10), I quoted Selwyn Hughes (1999) saying, "When 'a great number believed and turned to the Lord (v.21)', the Spirit of Christ was so evident that the people of Antioch could not help but notice the change in them. And since the characteristics of this group seemed similar to those of Jesus, they called them 'Christ's ones' – *Christians.*"

In the book cited in connection with Machovec (Ngara 2001b) I referred to the qualities of Jesus and commented: 'It is these qualities which have prompted a Marxist writer to say of Jesus the man "They (the disciples) saw in Him a man who already belonged to this coming Kingdom of God; they saw what it meant to be 'full of grace', what it meant to be not only a preacher but Himself the product of His teaching, a child of the future age to the marrow of His bones.'" I further made the comment that Machovec suggests that the Apostles were so loyal to Jesus precisely because His own person, His very being, was an embodiment of His message about the Kingdom of God (Machovec 1976:89-90). This kind of witness is amazingly surprising, coming from a Marxist who did not believe in God. It just shows the power and attractiveness of a Holy Spirit filled life that reflects and radiates the Kingdom of God. In his letter to the Romans, Paul comments about people who reflect the Kingdom of God in their lives: "For the Kingdom of God is not a matter of eating and drinking, but of righteousness, peace and joy in the Holy Spirit, because anyone who serves Christ in this way is pleasing to God and receives human approval" (Romans 14:17-18).

# Learning to lead for the Kingdom

The point of this discussion is to highlight the absolute necessity for the followers of Jesus of our time to re-orientate their lives so that they are more like the disciples in Antioch, the early Christians, and above all, like Jesus, their Master. The challenges the followers of Christ are facing today are not greater than the problems the early Christians encountered. The difference is in the inferior quality of our faith. Earlier on we quoted Henri Nouwen as saying it is not enough to try and imitate Christ as much as possible. The demand for us is to be "Living Christs here and now, in time and history" (Nouwen 2007:20). Thus our history demands of us to re-evaluate our orientation and practice as Christians so that we can be true citizens of the Kingdom of God, and in that way begin to seriously address the faith issues of our time. In this regard, it seems to me that Choo Thomas' book (2006) is a wake up call to us Christians to examine ourselves honestly and truthfully in relation to the Lord's Word to see whether we are the kind of disciples Jesus expects us to be; whether we are really true citizens of the Kingdom of God. It is when we have become true citizens of the Kingdom that we can face the problem of the scandalous divisions of our time. It is when we have resolved our own internal problems that we can address issues of competing religions, competing ideologies and secularism. But we cannot do these things on our own. We need the enlightenment and power of the Holy Spirit. We therefore, need to pray to the Holy Spirit to take possession of us.

## *A Special Message – Two Unique Challenges*

Before we leave the subject of lukewarm Christianity, I wish to refer very briefly to two challenges that might give the Church time to reinvent itself. The one is the glimmer of hope

# The Obligation and Power to Proclaim the Kingdom

that is reported in respect of the "underground church" in Islamic countries such as Syria, Iraq, Egypt and Somalia. In these countries, Muslims who dare to convert to Christianity are subjected to gruesome persecution and torture. They practice the Christian faith under conditions similar to the conditions the early Christians found themselves living under. In some of these countries, becoming a Christian is sentencing oneself to death. So, we have people who are being martyred for Jesus in the 21$^{st}$ century. In this regard, anyone interested in knowing the cruelty to which Muslims who convert to Christianity are subjected, should read Tom Doyle's fascinating book, *Killing Christians* (Doyle 2015).Two issues arise for me here: First, could this be another case of the more Christians are killed, the more Christianity grows? In other words, are we going to see a resurgence of Christianity in these countries? Second, it seems to me that believers in countries where there is freedom of worship have a duty to help these brothers and sisters in Christ. Assistance to these brothers and sisters in Christ could be included in any plan that may be developed to spread the gospel.

The second issue is that this book is being completed at a time when the Corona Virus (COVID-19) has negatively affected all human activities the world over. With regard to worship, for months now, it has not been possible for the faithful to go and pray in their Churches. The best many have to do is to listen to services over the radio or other media. Economically, the virus has had devastating effects on both companies and individual workers. As for working people, one is told many families are finding it difficult to make ends meet. I have also heard this has had negative effects on contributions to the upkeep of local Churches. I agree with those who suggest this is a time for the Church to reflect on what it means to be Church. When the world has finally managed to come out of the restrictions imposed by the virus, it will find itself facing many problems that are the result of this abnormal situation. Should the Church not find itself asking: What is the role of the Christian community in alleviating these problems? Is this not a time for Christians to come together and ask what is the Lord asking us to do as witnesses of Christ? Is it enough to pray for the victims of the virus, or is there something more significant that the churches can do together to help the world to see the Kingdom of God at work in the service of humanity?

It seems to me that both problems briefly summarized here, together with the others discussed in this chapter, should form part of a serious effort by the followers of Jesus to ask for the guidance of the Holy Spirit in regard to where the Church should be going at this point.

### Praying for the Guidance of the Holy Spirit

What should we do to receive the power of the Holy Spirit? At this point, I wish to focus on two things: First, we must hunger and thirst for baptism with the Holy Spirit. It is the power of the Holy Spirit that will give us the courage and enthusiasm to proclaim the Kingdom. RT Kendall (2014:134) has explained that baptism with the Holy Spirit includes at least three properties: power, illumination and cleansing. Our focus here is on the first two of these blessings. It was baptism with the Holy Spirit that gave the Apostles the power to proclaim Jesus as the risen Lord and Saviour of the world. And it was when the Holy Spirit descended on them that the disciples

# The Obligation and Power to Proclaim the Kingdom

became very clear in their own minds what the life, death and resurrection of Jesus were all about. They were now clear about the mission of Jesus, His suffering and His resurrection.

What we have just said above reminds us about John Stott's characterisation of the Holy Spirit as the searching, revealing, inspiring and enlightening Spirit (Stott 2002:59 ff). Applied to our present predicament in relation to where the Christian Church is now and our obligation to proclaim the Kingdom, we can say the following: The Holy Spirit will search for us what the will of God the Father is for us in this era; will reveal and clarify for us what the task is for the disciples of Jesus, and what the challenges are; will enlighten us on what we should do, and inspire us to proclaim the Kingdom with power and clarity of mind. The point of explaining all this is to say that one of the steps we must take to receive the baptism with the Holy Spirit, is to genuinely hunger and thirst for the power of the Holy Spirit.

The second thing that authorities on the subject say we should do, is to wait for the coming of the Holy Spirit. Says Andrew Murray (1984:148), "There must be a very definite waiting on God by the Holy Spirit to teach and lead us." This entails denial of self and surrender to the will of God. It also entails an understanding of the fact that understanding the workings of the Holy Spirit and consequently, receiving the power of the Holy Spirit, is not an intellectual activity or exercise. It involves the inner life. Andrew Murray (Ibid: 189 ff) has likened the make-up of a human being to the temple of the Old Testament. There was first an *outer court*, which every Israelite could enter; then there was the *Holy Place*, into which only the priests could enter; then there was the *Holy of Holies* which was the inaccessible abode of the Almighty. The Holy of Holies was only entered by the High Priest once a year.

Explaining Paul's exhortation to the Corinthians that they were "The temple of God" (1 Corinthians 3:16), Murray says that a human being is made up of three parts: *Body, Soul and Spirit.* The body is the visible component, equivalent to the outer court which is seen by everybody; the soul, with its power of mind, emotions and will is equivalent to the Holy Place; and the spirit, "the hidden, innermost sanctuary" is a spirit-nature "linking man with God." This is "the inner chamber of the heart" where the Spirit can come and dwell. In this way, the spirit of a human being is linked with God's Spirit. Consequently, what Paul says to the Corinthians: "Don't you know that you yourselves are God's temple and that God's Spirit dwells in your midst", applies equally to Christians of our time. However, for the Spirit to come and dwell in this secret chamber, we must prepare the chamber so that He can come and take possession of it. We must wait for the Spirit.

To ensure that the disciples were prepared and ready to receive and be baptized with the Holy Spirit, Jesus gave them this command: "Do not leave Jerusalem, but wait for the gift my Father has promised, which you have heard me speak about. For John baptized with water, but in a few days you will be baptized with the Holy Spirit" (Acts 1:4-5). The disciples clearly obeyed this command because Scripture tells us, "When the day of Pentecost came, they were all together in one place" (Acts 2:1). After the Last Supper and just before His suffering, Jesus had said to them, "But when he, the Spirit of truth, comes, he will guide you into all the truth" (John 16:13). And indeed, as we have just explained above, when the Spirit came on them on the Day of Pentecost, the Apostles were so enlightened, so inspired and so empowered, that they bravely and publicly explained the mission of Jesus to their audience, as can be seen in Peter's address (See Acts 2:14-41). The power of the Holy Spirit was such that He did not only empower Peter to deliver an eloquent speech, but that He also enlightened the hearts and minds of the Apostle's listeners to the extent that three thousand of the listeners received the message and were baptized.

There are lessons to be learned here by twenty-first century disciples of Jesus. First, as already explained, we must hunger and thirst for the power and guidance of the Holy Spirit. Second, we must learn to genuinely and sincerely wait for the coming of the Spirit on us. The impression one has is that in this fast society of our time, we are too much in a hurry to engage in whatever activity we decide to undertake. If we are gathered for a function, we have one of our Senior Clerics saying a short beautiful prayer at the beginning of the function; the rest of us answer "Amen", and we get down to business. What is suggested here is that there needs to be thorough preparation for whatever programmes we are going to undertake in order to address the faith issues of our time. In our next chapter, we endeavour to suggest the kind of preparation that can be made as well as the projects that can be undertaken.

Learning to lead for the Kingdom

# CHAPTER NINE

## Working together to Proclaim the Kingdom

### *Introduction: A Humble Lay Messenger's Testimony*

As I come to the last chapter of the book, this question haunts me: They will ask, "Who are you? On what authority do you say these things? Where did you get your training?" As a humble disciple of Jesus, a lay person burning with the desire to advance the cause of the Kingdom of God, I can only appeal to the authority of Scripture by referring to the following passages:

1.  "Am I now trying to win the approval of human beings, or of God?  Or am I trying to please people? If I were still trying to please people, I would not be a servant of Christ.

    I want you to know, brothers and sisters that the gospel I preached is not of human origin. I did not receive it from any man, nor was I taught it; rather I received it by revelation from Jesus Christ" (Galatians 1: 10-12).

2.  "And so it was with me, brothers and sisters. When I came to you, I did not come with eloquence or human wisdom as I proclaimed to you the testimony of God. For I resolved to know nothing while I was with you except Jesus Christ and him crucified. I came to you in weakness with great fear and trembling. My message and my

preaching were not with wise and persuasive words, but with a demonstration of the Spirit's power, so that your faith might not rest on human wisdom, but on God's power" (1 Corinthians 2: 1-5).

### *What Kind of Christians Ought We to Be?*

The purpose of this closing chapter is to urge the followers of Jesus to take practical action to advance the cause of the Kingdom of God in the Church and the temporal world, in time and history. The early Christians made a mark in their time. We are called upon to do the same in our own time. There is no doubt a lot is being done already. There are Churches and organisations that are doing their utmost to spread the Gospel of Christ – to take the Word to countries and places that are hostile to the message of Jesus and the Christian faith. We should acknowledge and applaud such work and the sacrifices that are being made by these foot soldiers of Christ, and by the denominations and organisations that support such activities. Having said that, it is necessary to also acknowledge the challenges and obligations discussed in earlier chapters and ask the question: If we are serious and faithful disciples of Jesus, can we say what is being done overall is enough? What should we do to ensure the Kingdom is more effectively proclaimed in our time?

Talking about the end of the world to the Christians of His time, who expected the imminent return of Christ, Peter asked, "Since everything is going to be destroyed in this way, what kind of people ought you to be?" (2 Peter 3:11). The question that might be appropriately addressed to the community of believers in our time is: If we are to proclaim the Kingdom as effectively as the early Christians did, what kind of people ought we to be? We should perhaps begin by going back to the apostolic times to hear what the Apostles and Jesus said about what kind of people Christians ought to be. Many books could be written on this subject. For our purposes in this chapter, we will focus on the following sets of verses:

### SET A: APOSTLES

(i)    Peter says, 'But just as he who called you is holy, so be holy in all you do; for it is written: "Be holy because I am holy" (1 Peter 1:15-16). Here, Peter is referring to Leviticus 11:44, 45; and Leviticus 19:2. In the latter text, the Lord tells Moses to say to the Israelites, 'Be holy because I, the LORD your God, am holy.'

(ii)    Peter also has this to say of Christians: "But you are a chosen people, a royal priesthood, a holy nation, God's special possession, that you may declare the praises of him who called you out of darkness into his wonderful light" (1 Peter 2:9).

(iii)    On his part James says this: "Religion that God our Father accepts as pure and faultless is this: To look after orphans and widows in their distress *and to keep oneself from being polluted by the world"* (James 1:27).

(iv)    Finally, Paul has this important message: "Do not conform to the pattern of this world, but be transformed by the renewing of your mind" (Romans 12:2).

# Learning to lead for the Kingdom

## SET B: JESUS

(i)    In the Sermon on the Mount, as explained in previous chapters, Jesus says, "You are the salt of the earth … You are the light of the world…" (Matthew 5:13-16).

(ii)    In the same sermon, He urges His followers to be unlike the rest of humanity and be like their Father in heaven: "Be perfect, therefore, as your heavenly Father is perfect" (Matthew 5:48).

(iii)    In His prayers before He is arrested He prays for His original disciples and for all believers: "My prayer is not that you take them out of the world but that you protect them from the evil one. They are not of the world, even as I am not of it… As you sent me into the world, I have sent them into the world" (John 17:15-18). This echoes the comment Jesus makes earlier to His disciples: "If you belonged to the world, it would love you as its own. As it is, you do not belong to the world, but I have chosen you out of the world. That is why the world hates you" (John 15:19).

(iv)    The next verse we shall quote is a continuation of the prayer just cited immediately above: "I pray also for those who will believe in me through their message, that all of them may be

one, Father, just as you are in me and I am in you
… I have given them the glory that you gave me,
that they may be one as we are one – I in them
and you in me – so that they may be brought to
complete unity. Then the world will know that
you sent me and have loved them as you have
loved me" (John 17:20-23).

(v)  Going hand in hand with the verse just quoted is
the following: "A new command I give you:
Love one another… By this everyone will know
that you are my disciples, if you love one
another" (John 13:34-35).

There are more scripture passages we could cite, but the
verses quoted here, are sufficient to clarify the relationship
between the followers of Jesus and the rest of humanity,
between "the world" and what we have called "the citizens of
the Kingdom." We are talking about guiding principles that
give uniqueness to "the citizens of the Kingdom."

1.  *The yardstick:* First, Kingdom citizens have a
    yardstick by which to measure their own priorities,
    behaviour, conduct and spirituality – their Father in
    heaven. They must be holy as their Father is Holy.
    They must be perfect as their Father in heaven is
    perfect. Achieving holiness and perfection is
    therefore, a major objective for all of them. Whatever
    they do, the yardstick is what they go by. As holiness
    is something to strive for, they should always be
    conscious of the fourth beatitude: "Blessed are those
    who hunger and thirst for righteousness, for they will
    be filled." They are consequently, "seekers of the
    kingdom", ever conscious of the injunction "But seek

first his kingdom and his righteousness, and all these things will be given to you as well" (Matthew 6:33).

Because of the above, Jesus' followers are "a chosen people, a royal priesthood, a holy nation, God's special possession." This harks back to the creation narrative in Genesis when God created humans "in his own image" and put them on planet earth to rule creation on His behalf. Just as humankind was originally intended to rule the world on God's behalf so that all creation would give glory to Him under the leadership of humans, the disciples of Jesus are supposed to "Declare the praises of him who called them out of darkness into his wonderful light." They have the capacity to do this because they are "a holy nation" and "a royal priesthood" - they are citizens of "the Kingdom of God."

2. ***Standards and Norms of the Kingdom:*** Whereas the nations of the world have their own constitutions, laws and values, the universal Kingdom of God has its own requirements and values the citizens must abide by. Their constitution is the Bible. However, there is always a temptation to conform to the values, behaviours, conduct and aspirations of the world. While they may abide by the laws of their natural states, the majority of the citizens of these states are after things like wealth, power, earthly success, competitiveness, etc. They hunger after these things: being a millionaire, owning the best house in town, possessing the latest model of the most prestigious car, being a super star, a popular singer, etc. These things become objectives in themselves. And citizens of the Kingdom are tempted to go along and

conform to these same values. As they are striving to seek the Kingdom, they may be distracted by such concerns and become polluted. They may be so steeped in the values of the world that their consciences are blunted and they may not even be conscious of the conflict between the values of the world and those of the Kingdom.

In view of all this, Paul says, "Do not conform to the pattern of this world, but be transformed by the renewing of your mind." And James advises, citizens of the Kingdom should "keep themselves from being polluted by the world." The Bible is our constitution which guides us in what is right and what is wrong. As Paul says to Timothy, "All Scripture is God-breathed and is useful for teaching, rebuking, correcting and training in righteousness, so that the servant of God may be thoroughly equipped for every good work" (2 Timothy 3: 16-17).

3. **In *the World but not* of *the World*:** Related to the standards and norms of the Kingdom is the fact that the disciples of Jesus are *in* the world but not *of* the world. As explained earlier, they have a virtual dual citizenship. They should abide by the laws of their natural states, but guided by the norms and values of the Kingdom. They have an obligation to participate in the development of their countries and the betterment of humanity, but always conscious of and guided by the standards and norms of the Kingdom. Their status as citizens of the world is in a sense a virtual one to the extent that when it comes to making a choice between obeying the world and

obeying the values and dictates of the Kingdom, they are expected to choose the latter.

Under normal circumstances, there is no necessary conflict between the world and the Kingdom, but there is always potential tension between the two. There are indeed times when the conflict between the demands of the world and the requirements of the Kingdom becomes real, and in these circumstances, some citizens of the Kingdom may find themselves in a real dilemma, and this is where their priorities and loyalty are put to the test. As we have seen, some Roman emperors persecuted Christians and even decreed that they be worshipped by the followers of Jesus. Many Christians chose to remain loyal to Jesus and consequently lost their lives as martyrs. They found themselves having to decide which citizenship was virtual and which was real. They were mindful of the Lord's words, "For whoever wants to save their life will lose it, but whoever loses their life for me and for the gospel will save it" (Mark 8:35). To these followers of Jesus, their true and real citizenship was in the Kingdom of God. A careful reading of Peter's First Letter will show that he was encouraging the Christians of his time to regard themselves as "foreigners and exiles" who were aware of the discrepancy between their Christian values and the values of the secular world in which they lived. Such discrepancies may not be very clear or even apparent to the majority of 21st century Christians.

In the 21st century, the majority of Christians practice their faith in conditions of relative freedom in this transitional phase of the Kingdom; but as noted in Chapter 8, there are many in some Islamic countries right now, in our time and age, who are having to make the difficult choice between Christianity and Islam. Once again, I encourage my readers to read Tom Doyle's book, *Killing Christians*. A related issue in regard to this is that if the citizens of the Kingdom in our time make a greater effort to proclaim the Kingdom, they may find themselves facing conditions similar to those the early Christians suffered under. This leads to the question: Under what conditions is the *true* Christian faith likely to grow? Is it likely to grow in our present circumstances when the majority of believers enjoy freedom of worship? I believe the Kingdom of God will manifest more clearly in this world when believers begin to show more effectively that they are *in* this world but not *of* this world.

4. ***Being Salt and Light:*** Instead of conforming to the patterns of the world, and instead of allowing themselves to be polluted by the world, the citizens of the Kingdom are meant to be "the salt of the earth" and "the light of the world" (Matthew 5: 13-16). While they are not *of* the world, they are nevertheless *in* the world and must impact it positively. As salt, they should aim to impact the world with the values of the Kingdom in such a way that the Kingdom grows like a mustard seed that is the smallest of all seeds but grows and becomes the largest of garden plants and even turns into a tree so that birds come and perch in its branches. As the salt of the earth, they should work like yeast that a woman mixed with flour until it worked "all through the dough" (Matthew 13:31-33). Note how the mustard seed and the yeast work – gently, quietly and gradually, but with a big bang at the end of the process. The method

is gentle and gradual, but the impact is great and powerful.

The Kingdom Jesus preached is a Kingdom of peace. Similarly, the citizens of the Kingdom are people of peace. They do not force the values of the Kingdom down people's throats. They understand the meaning of positive influence in leadership. A person of influence attracts people to themselves by their character, their manner, their integrity; by the way they deal with and treat other people. Their leader, Jesus, was a man of great influence; and He wanted His followers to impact the world the way salt flavours the food we eat. But He had a big warning for His followers: If salt loses its saltiness, the only thing to be done with it is "to be thrown out and trampled underfoot." This should lead us to ask: How salty are we? Are we salty enough not to deserve to be trampled underfoot?

A world without light is a world of darkness, and in darkness there is no life. John the evangelist says of Jesus, "In him was life, and that life was the light of the world" (John 1:4). John goes on to say, "The true light that gives light to everyone was coming into the world" (John 1:9). Let us consider what is happening here: Jesus is *the* light of the world, but He has bestowed the honour of being the light of the world to His followers. What an honour! This justifies Henri Nouwen's argument that it is not sufficient for us to be "like Christ", to imitate Christ as much as possible; we must rather be "living Christs" (Nouwen 2007:20). But with that great honour comes an equally major responsibility: "In the same way, let your light shine before others, that they may see your good deeds and glorify your Father in heaven." By what we do and by the way we live we reveal Christ, the light of the world to the world, to the glory of our Father in heaven.

As indicated several times before, the symbols of salt and light represent the leadership role that the followers of Jesus must play. That leadership role is not necessarily played by taking over the instruments of government, but by seasoning like salt the way the world works, and by holding the light that shows the way forward. How do we do this? Among other things, we submit ourselves to the rulers of our natural states, and being exemplary in all we do: "Live such good lives among the pagans that, though they accuse you of doing wrong, they may see your good deeds and glorify God on the day he visits us" (1 Peter 2:12). This, however, does not mean that we should be passive spectators where people are unjustly treated by oppressive and unjust rulers. As discussed in Chapter 3, citizens of the Kingdom should be promoters of justice, peace, good governance and a social system that is free of corruption.

5.  *In the Footsteps of the Master:* If we are to effectively proclaim and propagate the Kingdom in our circumstances, we will need to learn how to do our job from the Master Himself and heed His advice that He has set us an example, pointing out that the messenger is not greater than the one who sent Him (See John 13:15-16). In this regard, we should be mindful of Jesus' character and how He conducted Himself as a leader. We list here the characteristics we highlighted earlier:

(i)      His commitment to fulfil the Father's mission.

(ii)    Jesus as a faithful follower of the Father. This reminds us we should be faithful followers of Jesus our leader.

(iii)    His close relationship with and dependence on the Holy Spirit.

(iv)    His humility – the downward mobility principle which also reminds us that we should be prepared to take up our own cross and follow Him.

(v)    Courage in the face of adversity and opposition: A time will come - and indeed has come for some - when we have to demonstrate the courage of our convictions.

(vi)    Being an exemplary leader who walked his talk. Our mission is such that we do not only have to proclaim the Kingdom, but must demonstrate by our deeds and character that we are Kingdom people.

(vii)    Jesus was an exemplary servant leader, and He instituted the practice of servant leadership so that we may do to one another and to the world what He did for us.

6. ***Recognised through Unity in Plurality:*** The last passages we shall comment on here are (iv) and (v) under Set B. The first of these comes from John 17: 20-23, and the second from John 13: 34-35. These two are extremely important in relation to our effectiveness as witnesses of Christ. The first is about the world recognising Jesus as having been sent by the Father. If His followers are one, "Then the world will know that you sent me..." (John 17:23). Thus a

condition for the world recognising Jesus as the Messiah is the unity of His disciples. The second is about the world recognising the believers as His disciples: "By this everyone will know that you are my disciples, if you love one another." As explained before, it is our love for one another that will make the world see that we are Jesus' disciples. Love is our trade mark. In the absence of that love people won't even recognise us as Jesus' messengers, and if they can't recognise us as His followers, how can we then preach Him to them? There is a further point to note about the John 13 verse. Jesus is not just expressing a wish for His disciples to love one another: It is a *command*: "A new command I give you: Love one another." The message should really jog our consciences if we recall how in the past we have shown hostility to one another and even killed one another in the name of Jesus.

These verses sometimes lead me to think that at times we followers of Jesus do not seriously reflect on our Saviour's message and His instruction to us – that we are inclined to turn a blind eye to these messages, and are instead inclined to respect our denominations, traditions and theology more than we respect Jesus and the Bible. How can we be so slow in working for unity and Christian love when the Lord is so categorical about their importance to Him? Do we not see the harm caused to the task of evangelisation by our ignoring of Jesus' own pronouncements and instruction? When we read the command about the need to love one another, do we not open our ears to hear Jesus also saying, "Anyone who loves me will obey my teaching", and "Anyone who does not love me will not obey my teaching?" (John 14: 23-24).

When I find myself thinking like this, I am then forced to check myself by reflecting on the facts as far as I know them as a lay Christian: First, some of the divisions came about as a result of genuine concern about the message of the Bible. Second, the divisions are real and the differences in the interpretation of the Bible cannot be easily brushed aside. What is more, attitudes have not sufficiently changed to enable theologians to go forward in search of unity at a rate that some of us would like to see. Third, while the pace of ecumenism definitely seems to have slowed down, there is a lot that has been achieved by some Churches. An example of this is the Joint Declaration on the Doctrine of Justification signed in 1999 by the Lutheran World Federation and the Catholic Church. This was a major leap forward in narrowing the gap in agreement between Lutherans and Catholics. And this is only one example.

I was reflecting on these issues while writing this chapter when it suddenly dawned on me that I should find out what people say about Mahatma Gandhi's comments on Jesus and Christians. I searched on the internet for Mahatma Gandhi's sayings on Christianity. I found a number but was particularly struck by the following:
(i)     "Jesus is ideal and wonderful, but you Christians – you are not like Him."
(ii)    "It is a first class human tragedy that people of the earth who claim to believe in the message of Jesus, whom they describe as the

# Working together to Proclaim the Kingdom

Prince of Peace, show little of that belief in
actual practice."
(iii)   "Live like Jesus did, and the world will listen."
(iv)   "I'd be a Christian, if it were not for
Christians."

I was stunned and filled with sadness. I was
particularly moved by an article by Lama Chuck
Stanford and Arvind Khetia which is supposed to have
appeared in *Voices of Faith* under the heading "Why did
Gandhi say 'If it weren't for Christians, I'd be a
Christian.'" Briefly, the article tells the story of
Mahatma Gandhi visiting a Christian Church in
Calcutta one Sunday morning. He was not allowed to
enter because the Church was for high-caste Indians
and whites. Gandhi was neither high-caste nor white,
and so he could not enter. He then turned his back on
Christianity. The article says it was in this context that
Gandhi said, "I'd be a Christian if it were not for
Christians." I was then compelled to look up and quote
a comment I had read in R.T.Kendall's book, *Holy Fire:*
"The world will never know what might have been – if
only Mahatma Gandhi had run into Spirit-filled
Christians who demonstrated total forgiveness and
praying for their enemies. That is what Gandhi was
looking for." (Kendall 2014:164). Gandhi had such a
big impact on India. Had he become a Christian would
India still be one of the least evangelised countries of
the world?

In the same article in which I learned about
Gandhi turning his back on Christianity, I met the
Buddhist saying, "Don't confuse the finger pointing at

217

the moon for the moon itself." My comment here is: If I am looking for the moon and the only finger pointing at the moon is pointing in the wrong direction, will I ever be able to see the moon? Worse still, if there are a thousand fingers all claiming to be pointing at the moon but each finger pointing in a different direction from the others, how on earth am I expected to know which finger may be correctly pointing at the moon? And how can I ever hope to see the moon in such a confused state of affairs?

This is the lesson that we who call themselves Christians must learn about what we are doing to the world and the Lord Jesus. Our several thousand fingers are pointing in different directions and it is not easy for the people of the world to see their Saviour. Would we at least agree that our several thousand fingers should point in the same direction that the world may see Jesus and learn to know that the Father "So loved the world that he gave his one and only Son, that whoever believes in him shall not perish but have eternal life" (John 3:16). In promising the coming of the Holy Spirit Jesus told His disciples, "When he comes, he will prove the world to be in the wrong about sin and righteousness and judgment: about sin, because people do not believe in me..." (John 16: 8-9). This, then, is the sin of the world, that it does not believe in the Son sent by the Father to redeem it.

The comment about the sin of the world is important for ecumenism and Christian unity. When we, in our denomination or group of denominations, cling to our own position and refuse to cooperate with

# Working together to Proclaim the Kingdom

others whose theology is different from ours, we are concerned about the purity of theology or dogma. We may also feel resentment against other denominations or groups because of what we have done to each other in the past. I would make bold to argue that what we are forgetting here, is that, not only are we not obeying Jesus, but we are also in a sense participating in the sin of the world. We tend to conceive of Christian disunity as only a denomination to denomination matter, or as a Christian group to another Christian group matter. We do not seem to see its negative impact on non-believers. This is where we need to pray to the Holy Spirit that we may forget about our own positions and be humble enough to see that it is not we and our Churches and theology who matter most in this tragic conflict, but the rejected Christ, the world that rejects Him and the implications for unsaved souls.

I find statements by two authorities relevant to quote here: Andrew Murray (1984: 117 ff) has some useful insights to share in this regard. First, he talks about two marks that the work of the Spirit bears when he convinces us of the sin of the world: "One is the sacrifice of self, in the jealousy for God and His Honour, combined with the deep and tender grief for the guilty. The other is a deep strong faith in the possibility and power of deliverance." (119-120). These remarks are echoed by Cardinal Walter Kasper (2003:203-204) when he says, "Instead of demanding that our partners take steps in our direction that their conscience does not yet allow them to take, we should be the first to reflect on how we might move in their direction – and our steps may give them the courage to set out toward us."

# Learning to lead for the Kingdom

In our discussions with one another about theological issues, we therefore need to be prepared to sacrifice our own positions for the sake of God, that He may be honoured by the world. Guided by that level of spirit and humility, we should be able to see the world which does not believe in Jesus being convinced of its sin of disbelief and coming to believe in the Saviour of the world. Murray also says, among other things, that the rejected Christ has left the world and gone to the Father, "But He has left His people in it, and dwells in them by His Spirit, so that their holy life and their confession of Him may convince the world of its sin" (123). We are therefore, messengers and soldiers of Christ bearing the message of salvation and fighting for the manifestation of the Kingdom of God in our world. We do this more effectively when we present a united front despite our internal differences and disagreements.

But "the sacrifice of self in the jealousy for God and His Honour" does not necessarily imply prematurely abandoning our theological positions and traditions. Cardinal Kasper (2003:201) has suggested that "We must be content with doing what is possible and necessary today, looking to the great goal of visible unity and confident that it will be attained." But what is possible and necessary today without prematurely abandoning theological positions and traditions? We attempt to address this in the next section.

# Working together to Proclaim the Kingdom

## *Some Ways of Working Together*

*Aspects of Ecumenism that May Need More Attention*

We have now come to a point where a lay writer such as I am should not dare say anything. Christian Churches have the experience of working together and understand what is possible and what is not possible at this stage of the ecumenical movement, and how best to work together. Nevertheless, I believe as a lay disciple I can make some observations about what I have experienced as an interested party, and express some ideas that may add to the richness of the efforts that are being made to move towards gradual unity. I make the following points:

- First, it seems to me that the debate on ecumenism and Christian unity is focused principally at theological, ecclesial and dogmatic issues. While these are the central issues that gave rise to the division of the Church, the coming together of Christians should go beyond theological and ecclesial issues. Changing minds and attitudes seems to me to be an important aspect of the process. As long as we remain fixed on ideas without including a change of heart, we will remain suspicious of each other and this will surely impact on how much we love each other.

- Related to the point just made, is the fact that lay people remain on the periphery of the process and may not even be aware of the strides that are being made by Church leaders to bring the churches together. In this regard, I wonder how many lay Catholics and Lutherans are aware of the Joint Declaration on the Doctrine of Justification signed in

1999. The fact that agreements of this nature are not made public to the generality of the faithful, has implications for who the church is. Is it only the Clergy? How does this relate to Paul's definition of the body of Christ: "For we were all baptized by one Spirit so as to form one body - whether Jews or Gentiles, slave or free – and we were all given the one Spirit to drink." And furthermore, "Now you are the body of Christ, and each one of you is a part of it" (1 Corinthians 12: 13, 27).

- It seems to me that the progress in resolving theological, doctrinal and ecclesial issues should be enforced by a greater effort to work together by holding services, prayer meetings and engaging in joint community and other activities without necessarily violating each other's positions on such texts as 1 Corinthians 10:16-17 which relates to the contentious issue of the joint celebration of the Eucharist. In the next section I comment on examples of working and praying together that I found inspiring.

## Two Examples of Working Together in Durban, South Africa

### THE DIAKONIA COUNCIL OF CHURCHES

The Diakonia Council of Churches brings together all Christian denominations in Durban. A particular case of working together by the churches that I wish to mention here, is the Ecumenical Good Friday Service. I believe in the ten and half years that my wife and I were working in Durban and

# Working together to Proclaim the Kingdom

living in the Westville suburb of the city, there was not one single year when this service did not take place. Because the different Churches would hold their own denominational services on the same day, the interdenominational service always started at 6 o'clock in the morning, early enough not to interfere with the times at which the different individual Churches or Parishes would hold their own.

In the interdenominational service, Christians would together commemorate the passion of their Lord Jesus Christ, praying, singing, listening to a sermon and engaging in other forms of devotion. For the greater part of the time when my wife and I were in Durban, the interdenominational service took place in the International Convention Centre. The most impressive part of the ceremony for me was the carrying of a cross in a procession that took the worshippers through the streets of Durban to the City Hall where final prayers would be said, with the cross being left in a prominent place outside the Hall. On the way to the City Hall, individuals would volunteer to take turns in carrying the cross. I never wanted to miss the interdenominational Good Friday Service because I found it to be a wonderful way of people of different denominations witnessing for Christ in a city where there are large populations of Hindus and Muslims. On this occasion, Anglicans, Baptists, Charismatics, Catholics, Evangelicals, Methodists, Pentecostals, Salvation Army members, members of the Zion Christian Church and other groups, found a common identity in the suffering Christ and together acknowledged Him as Lord and Saviour.

# Learning to lead for the Kingdom

## *THE CHRISTIAN PRACTICE FELLOWSHIP*

### *Composition of the Group*

The Diakonia Council of Churches is led by Church leaders. The Christian Practice Fellowship, which I led, was an initiative of lay Christians. Our original venue was our house until the Fellowship was given a room to work in by the Westville Methodist Church. The Fellowship, which had a formal constitution, brought together Anglicans, Catholics, Methodists and at least one Baptist who eventually converted to Methodism. This was the core group of the Fellowship, but members of other denominations were involved in its activities. The core group was small with less than thirty members if my memory serves me well. The Christian Practice Fellowship (originally the Christian Practice Movement) was short lived – its lifespan was something like five years or so – but in that short period, it had some achievements.

### *Aims*

Without access to the documents that guided the members, I can only try to recapture the aims of the group. As I recall, the basic aim of the Fellowship was to propagate the idea of closing the gap between faith and practice in Christianity. The members felt that Christianity had become a religion in which there was a glaring disjuncture between faith and practice. One of the ways in which this disjuncture manifested itself, was the division among Christians and the consequent lack of Christian love between the members of different denominations. It was therefore incumbent upon Christians to show that they could love one another and work together despite theological and other differences. Supporting ecumenical activities, praying together, studying the Bible and

224

# Working together to Proclaim the Kingdom

working together as a Christian community were some of the ways in which the Fellowship would seek to bridge the gap between faith and practice - without necessarily getting involved in theological and doctrinal debates that were the province of theologians and Church leaders. As lay believers, it was incumbent upon them to try and get support from their Pastors and Priests and Senior Church Leaders such as Bishops. Among the Senior Clergy who gave their support in one way or another, were: Bishop Rubin Phillip of the Anglican Church, Bishop Purity Malinga of the Methodist Church, and the late Catholic Archbishop of Durban, Denis Hurley (from whom I personally learnt much about ecumenism).

## Activities

The fact that we could meet together, discuss matters of faith and pray together was in itself some kind of success. We got so relaxed with one another that we could poke fun at each other's denominations without getting offended. In that kind of context, the word *papists* could be used without offending Catholics. But what I can count as "successes" of the Fellowship include the following:

1. The first major event was a *Walk for Christ* event which set Westville Suburb abuzz with people joining the walk which was a fundraising event combined with witnessing for Christ as well as having fun for the participants. As I remember, it was a five kilometre walk for which every participant paid R5 (five South African Rand) in support of the projects of the Fellowship. It was a very colourful event with the participants holding makeshift flags displaying the

cross and other Christian symbols. Young and old joined the walk, showing the Westville community that Jesus Christ was alive and members of different confessions could come together to show they believed in Him.

2. The second activities I would like to mention, were a couple of *Retreats* for members of the Fellowship and any other interested persons. The principle here was if the venue belonged to a particular denomination the pastor or priest invited to conduct the retreat had to be from a different denomination. I remember two of these retreats. The first was held at a YMCA centre whose manager was a prominent Assemblies of God woman, Dina Daniels, whom I remember as a beloved, open minded and deeply spiritual Christian. The retreat master was a Black Redemptorist Catholic priest from the Western Cape. He had been to Taize in France and part of the programme was to teach us to pray the way people pray at Taize. It was very inspiring. The second was held in a Catholic monastery at Marianhill outside Pinetown. The retreat master was an Anglican priest. There is a big church at Marianhill, but we were allowed to have our retreat in the Monastery chapel!

3. The third event was a *Conference* we organised for which the venue was the Westville Centre, a secular environment. This was quite a big event addressed by some very prominent people including two Anglican bishops. The late Archbishop Denis Hurley of the Catholic Archdiocese of Durban, a great supporter of the Christian Practice Fellowship, had intended to address the Conference, but was in the end not able

to attend in person. The Pastor/Parish Priest of each of the local Churches - Anglican, Baptist, Catholic and Methodist – had a role to play in the Conference. The activities included talks on ecumenism and a major Bible study session led by a Methodist Minister who took the participants through the Sermon on the Mount.

4. The next event had to do with the *Christian Unity Service* of one of the years of our existence. There used to be a Christian Unity Week each year, if my memory serves me right, and an interdenominational service would be held to pray for Christian unity. In one of the years in the early 2000s, the Christian Practice Fellowship was given the honour of organising the unity service under the guidance of a senior Anglican priest. We requested Bishop Purity Malinga, a female Methodist Bishop, to lead the service and to preach, and she kindly obliged. Bishop Malinga is now (at the writing of this book) the Presiding Bishop of the Methodist Church of Southern Africa.

I cannot speak for my colleagues in the Christian Practice Fellowship, but that community of genuine believers, true citizens of the Kingdom, has contributed very significantly to my growth as a Christian and a disciple of Jesus. It has opened my mind to the richness of the beliefs, practices and traditions of other denominations. As the years have gone by, and I have read books written by members of different Christian confessions, I have come to believe that the Lord is calling us to come together to read the Scriptures together and openly, and in a spirit of love, share what we believe in common and what each side believes about some of the parts of the Bible that divide us. The suggestions that are made in the next section are partly informed by this background.

## Some Suggestions for the Way Forward

Writing this conclusion has been a difficult task for a number of reasons: First, as already mentioned, there is much that Church leaders are doing which is unknown to me, and so my suggestions may be superfluous or too naïve to be useful. Second, as I have already stated, I have no authority to make any recommendations or suggestions save for the desire to see the commands of Jesus acted upon and a greater effort made to extend the Kingdom of God on earth. It is out of these convictions that I do not make recommendations, but put forward the following suggestions for consideration by people who hold positions of influence in Christian Churches. In my mind, I see the activities suggested here taking place at local/national, regional and international levels; as well as at denominational and interdenominational levels.

### 1. Interdenominational Meeting of Denominational Leaders and Theologians

This may already be taking place, but the suggestions made below are made on the assumption that such a meeting or meetings would take place to consider some of the ideas discussed in this book and this closing chapter. This may be a meeting of top level denominational leaders or representatives authorized to take decisions on behalf of their superiors. Specific groups that would need to be present in addition to the main players, would be the laity, women and the youth. The

# Working together to Proclaim the Kingdom

issues to be deliberated on are listed in item 3 below, on the understanding that issues would be amended as the authorities think appropriate.

## 2. Prayers to the Holy Spirit

It is envisaged that this would be the first activity after some initial preparation for it. It is envisaged that prayers to the Holy Spirit would be organised at local, regional and international levels to seek the guidance of the Paraclete in facing the challenges of our time. Due consideration would be given to the fact that the Holy Spirit needs to be waited for; that there should be a time for preparing our hearts and minds to receive the Spirit and to get His guidance.

## 3. Key Issues to be Deliberated Upon

It is recommended that when Heads of Denominations, theologians and others participating in the proposed international ecumenical gathering meet, they should spend a full day preparing to receive the revelation, inspiration and power of the Holy Spirit before the deliberations begin. This "waiting for the Spirit" could take the form of common prayers, Scripture readings, silent prayer, individual and group reflections, and an ecumenical service in which the Holy Spirit is invoked to come and guide the meeting. They should be gathered together like the disciples on the Day of Pentecost. Among the hymns that would be appropriate to sing at such an event is the ancient song *"Come, Holy Ghost, Creator, Come" (Veni, Creator Spiritus),* ascribed to one Rabanus Maurus who is thought to have lived in the years 776-856, long before the major divisions of the Church. The following are the topics

229

suggested for discussion and reflection at the gathering with any necessary amendments:

(i)      The Evangelisation of the world

(ii)     Ecumenism and Christian unity

(iii)    The challenges of Secularism

(iv)    Guidance to Kingdom Citizens on how to witness for Christ and spread Kingdom values in the following spheres:

- The family
- The work place
- Government structures
- The community of believers, and
- The broader community

(v)     Support for persecuted Christians.

The last mentioned may be a very sensitive issue as it may impact on relations between Christians and members of the religions concerned, and may expose Christians living under such conditions even more. It may therefore need to be handled carefully using an appropriate strategy. Discreet research could be conducted before the topic is discussed in full.

### Conclusion: Setting the World on Fire

We conclude with a reminder about Jesus' passion for the mission given to Him by the Father. His first message, as recorded in the synoptic Gospels, was to announce the Kingdom. Here we shall quote the Gospel of Mark: "'The time has come," He said. "The Kingdom of God has come near.

# Working together to Proclaim the Kingdom

Repent and believe the good news!'" (Mark 1:15). As stated earlier, zeal for the mission given to Him by the Father consumed Jesus. It was His mission that sustained Him as food sustains the rest of us: "'My food," said Jesus, "is to do the will of him who sent me and to finish his work'" (John 4:34). Such was His zeal for the mission that He wanted to set the world on fire with the news of the Kingdom: "I have come to bring fire on the earth, and how I wish it were already kindled!" (Luke 12:49). The fire was kindled on Pentecost Day. The early Christians kept it blazing. We Christians of the twenty-first century have the challenge of setting the earth ablaze with a strong awareness of the news of the Kingdom and Salvation through Evangelism, Ecumenism, challenging Secularism and Apostasy, supporting persecuted believers, and spreading the values of the Kingdom in all spheres of life.

Learning to lead for the Kingdom

## APPENDIX I: SOME TOPICS FOR A COURSE IN KINGDOM STUDIES

Kingdom Studies does not seem to be an important part of the training of Pastors, Priests and others who hold positions of influence in the Church. Any reader of this book and of the works of authors like Myles Munroe, should be able to get the message that training to ministry which excludes Kingdom studies is not entirely adequate, to say the least. In that regard, part of the original intention of this author was for the book to serve as a text that could be used for the training of people who hold positions of authority in the Church. As the theme developed, it then became somewhat inappropriate to disturb the flow of ideas by inserting training exercises at the end or beginning of each chapter as it now appeared necessary to include Church leaders as part of the readership of the book. It then seemed appropriate to have a list of topics that could be included in such a course as well as examples of exercises as appendices to the book.

The advantage of having the course as an appendix is that those readers who want to use the book as a textbook for students can do so, while those who just want to read the message in the book can do so without any interruption. There are two appendices, one on the topics that can be included in designing a Kingdom Studies course, and the other on the kind of exercises that would be appropriate for such a course. This first appendix is for the suggested topics. These are used only as guidelines for institutions that may want to design such a course. Some of these could be combined, and some replaced by other topics that may be considered more appropriate. The course could be designed for a postgraduate Diploma in Kingdom Studies, or it could be included as part of a degree programme. It should be up to each institution to decide the level at which the course should be taught.

The topics include the following:

1. The creation of the universe and the place of humankind in God's Kingdom on earth
2. The fall and Its consequences
3. The perpetual struggle between good and evil
4. God's preparation for the restoration of the Kingdom
5. The mission of Jesus' Christ with special reference to the Kingdom of God and Salvation for humankind
6. The fulfilment of the law and the Prophets by Jesus Christ
7. Jesus' teaching on the Kingdom in the following:
   (a) The Sermon on the Mount
   (b) The relevant parables
8. The teachings of Jesus, Paul and Peter on the end of the world and the coming of the reign of Christ
9. The first Kingdom of God on earth and the Kingdom of God in the New Heaven and the New Earth
10. The history and future of the Christian Church in relation to Schism, Ecumenism and Future Unity

# APPENDIX II: SOME TOPICS FOR A COURSE IN KINGDOM STUDIES

The exercises fall into three categories as follows:

(a) Written questions for assignments or even examinations

(b) Topics for debate by the students, and

(c) Personal testimonies. Testimonies compel students to think deeply about how the particular topic has impacted on them personally. Experience has shown that these are done in class with individual students volunteering to talk about themselves for a relatively short time in order to have time for all who want to speak to do so. Some students may not want to speak about themselves and should not be compelled to do so. In this regard, some may even want to share their experience privately with the lecturer in written form, and it would be appropriate to offer this opportunity to those who are inclined to do so.

A point that should be made here, is that the exercises are examples of the kind of questions and topics that can be used to help students to learn more about the Kingdom of God. Some lecturers may find it necessary to add more to these as long as such questions or topics are relevant to the theme of the book.

### Section A: Written Assignments

1. Summarise what *Learning to Lead for the Kingdom* presents as the three phases of the kingdom of God on earth, and comment on whether you agree or

# Learning to lead for the Kingdom

disagree partially or fully with the contents of the book, giving reasons for agreeing or disagreeing with the author.

2.  Comment on what is presented in the book about the characteristics of the middle (or second) phase of the Kingdom of God on earth, and say whether you agree or disagree, giving reasons for agreeing or disagreeing with the author.

3.  Read the following :

4.  (a) Relevant chapters of *Learning to Lead for the Kingdom*
    (b) Revelation Chapters 21 and 22
    (c) Isaiah 65:17-25
    Then write an essay on "The Final Stage of the Kingdom of God" based on these three readings.

5.  Read the following:
    (a)  Genesis Chapters 1-3
    (b)  Revelation Chapters 21-22
    (c)  Chapter 2 of John Eldredge's *All Things New*.

    Then write an essay on what these readings reveal about the transformation of the earth and human life at the end of the world.

6.  Write an essay on Jesus' conception of the Kingdom of God on earth based on "The Sermon on the Mount."

7.  Read the following verses:
    (a)Luke 14: 25-24
    (b) Luke 22:28-30
    (c) Matthew 26:27-29
    (d) Revelation 19: 7-9.
    Discuss what these verses have in common and say what they reveal about the kingdom of God in the New Earth at the time of Christ's Reign.

# APPENDIX II: SOME TOPICS FOR A COURSE IN KINGDOM STUDIES

8. Write an essay on the following: "Repentance and the Kingdom of God" and "Belief and Salvation" as themes in the Jesus' message. End your essay by commenting on what importance the followers of Jesus should attach to these two themes.

9. Write an essay on the role of the Holy Spirit in the Life of Jesus and the importance that should be attached to the Spirit by teachers of the Bible and followers of Jesus.

10. "Servant Leadership as taught and practised by Jesus is not given the importance it deserves in the teaching and practice of the Christian Church today." Discuss.

11. Read C. Gene Wilkes' *Jesus on Leadership* and say to what extent it has made you understand Jesus' teaching on servant leadership.

12. "Every ordained minister of the Church should take the vow of servant leadership as taught and practiced by Jesus." Discuss.

### *Section B: Topics for Debate*

1. Team A: Christianity will remain the largest religion of the world throughout the 21st Century and beyond.
   Team B: Islam will take over Christianity as the largest religion of the world by 2070.

2. Team A: It is important for Christians of all major denominations to come to an agreement on all important theological, doctrinal and ecclesial matters before Christian unity can be achieved.
   Team B: It is necessary for Christians to show love to one another and ability to work together before unity can be achieved.

3.  Team A: Real Christian unity means having one Church.

    Team B: Christian unity can only be achieved if there is agreement on unity in plurality.

4.  Team A: The Kingdom of God will be made manifest to the world when Christians are able to come together to the table of the Lord and participate in the Eucharist as one community sharing the body of Christ as one in belief.

    Team B: The Kingdom of God will be made manifest to the world when, despite differences in their understanding of the Eucharist, Christians will come together, worship the Lord together, and even have Holy Communion in different groups according to their beliefs, but end the service together as followers of Jesus.

5.  Team A: The greatest challenge facing the Christian Church in our time, is to be able to preach the Gospel to all nations, including those that are hostile to the Christian faith.

    Team B: The greatest challenge facing Christianity in our time is the ability to demonstrate that it is a superior religion in terms of the character and behaviour of its adherents, and in terms of the relationship between faith and practice.

### Section C: Individual Testimonies

1.  My concept of the Kingdom of God before I read *Learning to Read for the Kingdom*, and my understanding of the idea now.

238

# APPENDIX II: SOME TOPICS FOR A COURSE IN KINGDOM STUDIES

2. My understanding of the Lord's Prayer before I enrolled for this course, and my understanding of the prayer now.
3. What the course has taught me about the Kingdom of God and my purpose in life.
4. My journey as a disciple of Jesus.
5. My view of the Church of tomorrow.
6. How my life has been changed by the Bible.
7. My favourite book of the Bible.
8. The book that has had the greatest impact on me in addition to the Bible.
9. My view of today's Christianity compared with that of the early Christians.

# Learning to lead for the Kingdom

# References

Amaral, J.(2011) *Understanding JESUS: Cultural Insights into the Words and Deeds of Christ.* New York, Boston, Nashville: Faith Words.

Anderson, L. (1999) *Leadership That Works: Hope and Direction for Church and Parachurch Leaders in Today's Complex World.* Minneapolis, Minnesota: Bethany House Publishers.

Bailey, B. (2018) *Learning to Lead Like Jesus.* Eugene, Oregon: Harvest House Publishers.

Bellitto, C.M. (2008) *Church History 101: A Concise Overview.* Missiouri:Liguouri.

Blanchard, K.& Hodges, P. *Lead Like Jesus: Lessons for Everyone From the Greatest Leadership Role Model of All time.* Nashville, Tennessee: Thomas Nelson.

Bloomer, J. (1995) *Authority Abusers: Breaking Free from Spiritual Abuse.* New Kensington: Whitaker House.

Boehme, R. (1989) *Leadership for the 21st Century: Changing Nations through the Power of Serving.* Seattle, Washington: YWAM Publishing.

Booth, Edwin P. (MCMXCV) *Martin Luther: The Great Reformer.* Uhrichsville: Barbour and Company Inc.

Buford, B. (1994) *Half Time: Changing Your Game Plan from Success to Significance.* Grand Rapids, Michigan: Zondervan.

Eusebius (Trans G.A.Williams) (1965, 1989) *The History of the Church.* London: Penguin Books.

# Learning to lead for the Kingdom

Frankl, Viktor, E. *Man's Search for Meaning.* New York, London etc: Pocket Books.

De Caussade, J.P. (Trans H.M. Helms) *The Joy of Full Surrender.* Bandra, Mumbai: St Pauls.

Doyle, T. (2015) *Killing Christians: Living the Faith Where it's Not Safe to Believe.* Nashville, Tennessee: William Publishing Group.

Eldredge, J.(2017)  *All Things New: Heaven, Earth and the Restoration of Everything You Love.* Nashville, Tennessee: Nelson Books..

Getz, Gene A. (2000) *Paul: Living for the Call of Christ:* Nashville: Tennessee: Broadman & Holman Publishers.

Hendriksen,W. (1940, 1967, 2015) *More Than Conquerors: An Interpretation of Revelation.* Grand Rapids, Michigan: BakerBooks.

Hindson, E D, & Hitchcock M (2017) *Can We Still Believe in the Rapture?* Eugene, Oregon: Harvest House Publishers.

### *Holy Bible, The*

*The New Jerusalem Bible.* London: Darton.Longman and Todd (2002).

NRSV Bible: *With Apocryphal / Deuterocanonical Books New Revised Standard Version*
Glasgow, London, New York etc: Collins Publishers (1989).

Johnson, B. (2013) *When Heaven Invades Earth: Expanded Edition.* Shippensburg: Destiny Image ® Publishers, Inc.

Johnson B. (2019) *The Resting Place: Living Emmersed in the Presence of God.* Shippensburg: Destiny ®Image Publishers

# References

Kasper W. Cardinal (2003) *Leadership in the Church: How Traditional Roles can Serve the Christian Community Today.* New York: The Crossroad Publishing Company.

Keene, M (2002) *Christianity.* Oxford: Lion Publishing plc.

LaHaye,T. & Hindson, E. (2015) *Target Israel.* Eugene, Oregon: Harvest House Publishers.

Lead and Inspire School of Leaderhip (2010) **Foundations of Christian Leadership: The Facilitator's Manual.** Pretoria: Unpublished Teaching Materials.

Lewis, C.S. (1944) *Mere Christianity.* London: William Collins.

Loney, C. (2003) *Heroic Leadership: Best Practices from a 450-Year Old Company that Changed the World.* Chicago, Illinois: Loyola Press.

Machovec, M.(1976) *A Marxist Looks at Jesus.* Philadelphia: Fortress Press.

Mayhew McCrimmon (1988) *The Complete Celebration Hymnal: with New Songs for Celebration.* Great Wakering, Essex: McCrimmons.

McDowell, J. & Bellis, David H.(2006) *The Last Christian Generation.* Holiday, Florida: Green Key Books.

Mundakel, T.T. (2003) *Blessed Mother Teresa.* London: Simon &Schuster/Townhouse.

Munroe, M (2006) *Kingdom Principles: Preparing for Kingdom Experience and Expansion.* Shippensburg: Destiny Image Publishers.

Munroe, M (2010) *Rediscovering the Kingdom: Expanded Edition: Ancient Hope for Our 21ˢᵗ Century:* Shippensburg: Destiny Image Publishers.

Ngara, E. (2001a) *Come, Follow Me: A Call to Discipleship and Christian Practice.* Muckleneuk, Pretoria: CB Powell Bible Centre, UNISA.

Ngara, E. (2001b) *The Kingdom of God and Christian Life: Towards a New Ethos for the Followers of Jesus. Muckleneuk, Pretoria: CB Powell Bible Centre, UNISA.*

Ngara, E. (2004) *Christian Leadership: A Challenge to the African Church.* Nairobi: Paulines Publications Africa.

Ngara, E. (2019) *Learning to Lead for a Better World:* Wandsbeck, South Africa: Emmanuel Ngara with Reach Publishers.

Nolan, A. (1976, 1992) *Jesus Before Christianity:* Maryknoll, New York: Orbis Books.

Nouwen, H. (2007) *The Selfless Way of Christ: Downward Mobility and the Spiritual Life.* Maryknoll, New York: Orbis Books.

Stott, J. (2007) *Calling Christian Leaders: Biblical models of church, gospel and ministry.* Leicester, England: Inter-Varsity Press.

Thomas, C. (2006) *Heaven Is So Real!* Cape Town: Struik Christian Media.

Warren, R. (2002) *The Purpose Driven Life: What on Earth Am I Here For ?* Grand Rapids, Michigan: Zondervan.

Wright, B. (2017) *The Stage Is Set.* Grand Rapids, Michigan:BakerBooks.

# References

Zimbabwe Catholic Bishops Conference (2012) *Tinokutendai Mambo: Dzimbo dzeKirike Katolike 1962-2011.* Life Lines: Dominican Missionary Sisters of the Sacred Heart of Jesus.

Lead and Inspire School of Leaderhip (2010) **Foundations of Christian Leadership: The Facilitator's Manual.** Pretoria: Unpublished Teaching Materials.

Lewis, C.S. (1944) *Mere Christianity.* London: William Collins.

Loney, C. (2003) *Heroic Leadership: Best Practices from a 450-Year Old Company that Changed the World.* Chicago, Illinois: Loyola Press.

Machovec, M.(1976) *A Marxist Looks at Jesus.* Philadelphia: Fortress Press.

Mayhew McCrimmon (1988) *The Complete Celebration Hymnal: with New Songs for Celebration.* Great Wakering, Essex: McCrimmons.

McDowell, J. & Bellis, David H.(2006) *The Last Christian Generation.* Holiday, Florida: Green Key Books.

Mundakel, T.T. (2003) *Blessed Mother Teresa. London: Simon &Schuster/Townhouse.*

Munroe, M (2006) *Kingdom Principles: Preparing for Kingdom Experience and Expansion.* Shippensburg: Destiny Image Publishers.

Munroe, M (2010) *Rediscovering the Kingdom: Expanded Edition: Ancient Hope for Our 21st Century:* Shippensburg: Destiny Image Publishers.

Ngara, E. (2001a) *Come, Follow Me: A Call to Discipleship and Christian Practice*. Muckleneuk, Pretoria: CB Powell Bible Centre, UNISA.

Ngara, E. (2001b) *The Kingdom of God and Christian Life: Towards a New Ethos for the Followers of Jesus. Muckleneuk, Pretoria: CB Powell Bible Centre, UNISA.*

Ngara, E. (2004) *Christian Leadership: A Challenge to the African Church*. Nairobi: Paulines Publications Africa.

Ngara, E. (2019) *Learning to Lead for a Better World:* Wandsbeck, South Africa: Emmanuel Ngara with Reach Publishers.

Nolan, A. (1976, 1992) *Jesus Before Christianity:* Maryknoll, New York: Orbis Books.

Nouwen, H. (2007) *The Selfless Way of Christ: Downward Mobility and the Spiritual Life*. Maryknoll, New York: Orbis Books.

Stott, J. (2007) *Calling Christian Leaders: Biblical models of church, gospel and ministry*. Leicester, England: Inter-Varsity Press.

Thomas, C. (2006) *Heaven Is So Real!* Cape Town: Struik Christian Media.

Warren, R. (2002) *The Purpose Driven Life: What on Earth Am I Here For?* Grand Rapids, Michigan: Zondervan.

Wright, B. (2017) *The Stage Is Set.* Grand Rapids, Michigan:BakerBooks.

Zimbabwe Catholic Bishops Conference (2012) *Tinokutendai Mambo: Dzimbo dzeKirike Katolike 1962-2011*. Life Lines: Dominican Missionary Sisters of the Sacred Heart of Jesus.

# ABOUT THE AUTHOR

Professor Emmanuel Ngara, a distinguished academic, prolific writer and former diplomat, and the Lord elevated him from his illustrious career in academia and university executive leadership to focus on the training of leaders and to transform believers through his written work. His first book-length publication on leadership, Christian Leadership: A Challenge to the African Church (Paulins Publications Africa), featured a foreword by Archbishop Desmond M. Tutu, Anglican Archbishop Emeritus of Cape Town.

STAY CONNECTED WITH PROF EMMANUEL NGARA

Email: professor.e.a.ngara@gmail.com

Tel: +27 82 665 8001